GLOUCES⁣ ⁣SHIRE HERITAGE WALKS

John Abbott

ROSE . W .

Published by Sigma Leisure – an imprint of
Sigma Press, 1 South Oak Lane, Wilmslow, Cheshire SK9 6AR, England.

British Library Cataloguing in Publication Data
A CIP record for this book is available from the British Library.

ISBN: 1-85058-393-5

Typesetting and Design by: Sigma Press, Wilmslow, Cheshire.

Cover design: Martin Mills

Printed in Malta by
Interprint Ltd.

Acknowledgments

I would like to thank David Medcroft
for taking, developing and printing the photographs
and the Stewarts – Nancy, John and Duncan – for their support.

Contents

Background Readings
on Rural Gloucestershire

Location Map

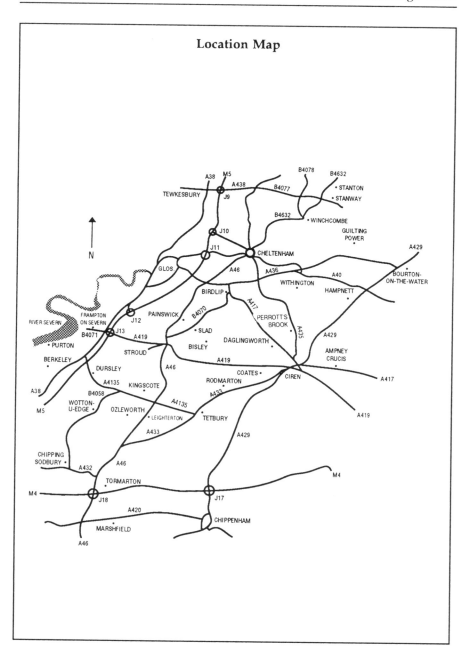

Introduction

This book describes twenty-five walks in glorious Gloucestershire; the 'old' Gloucestershire, ignoring the shifting county boundaries of the past few years. Currently, two are in upstart Avon, one straddles both counties, while another, the Bourton walk, includes a section along the Oxfordshire Way; in Gloucestershire, this time.

The theme is history: churches, in particular; each walk includes at least one church with, where necessary, a description of the main features. Other places of interest to walker and visitor alike are also mentioned: hill forts, long barrows, a Roman villa, a private railway, a butterfly farm.

A sketch map is included with each walk, though these are no substitute for the Ordnance Survey maps of the area. Their Landranger or Pathfinder series are recommended since they give a clear 'picture' of the terrain – contour lines, directions, general features – to be covered.

Many of the walks include long/short options and range from easy to quite demanding. Dursley to Hetty Pegler's Tump, for example, with its three testing ascents: Cam Peak, Cam Long Down and the 'killer' to the top of Crawley Hill. If you are new to walking, like any activity, it is wise to pace yourself, building stamina as you progress. Obviously, do not attempt the Dursley walk at 'full throttle' if your previous walking experience is ten minutes through the local park.

Dress sensibly, and not only with the weather in mind. Light clothing, warm in the winter, cool in the summer, that protects from brambles and nettles. Take a waterproof; even during a drought; even if only in the car. Weather forecasts have been known to be wrong. Boots that have been worn a few times, proven 'blister free', are recommended. Woollen socks are a good idea, as well. I do most of my walking from early autumn through to late spring, avoiding the hot(?) summer months, so you may notice the occasional reference to mud.

I apologise in advance should you find that a walk does not correspond with my description. Proof-reading errors are my fault, entirely. Additionally, you may have to cope with the sticky clay of freshly ploughed fields, waist-high crops, new stiles, gates, fences, even a change of route – anything can happen, and sometimes does. May, in particular, is a month of fantastic growth and change – a mix of sun, rain and footpaths full of long, wet grass. Church and other detail, too, can change – a restoration, a rearrangement – again, my apologies.

Unfortunately, it is not easy (sometimes impossible) to get to the start of a walk and home again without some form of transport of your own. I have included notes for the motorist – getting there, parking – and added a word or two on buses, often nothing more than a telephone number. The problem is that many of today's bus routes in the country are privately run – operators and times may vary from year to year.

Above all, enjoy the walks. Why not do each one several times? It is surprising what can be missed the first time around when one is looking out for that elusive arrow-head.

So there you are, ready to go, and the rain comes down. To pass the time (for it will stop, eventually), why not 'dip into' the three articles at the end of the book? The titles speak for themselves.

1. Wotton-under-Edge to Hawkesbury Upton

Mentioned in the Saxon Royal Charter of 940 AD, the then 'Wudu tun', or farm in the wood, has had a long and sometimes bloody history: the feuds of the powerful Berkeley family, King John's tyranny and his reported burning of the town. A new one emerged from the ashes of the old, to grow and prosper from a thriving wool trade. The Wotton-under-Edge of today is a mixture of local industry and a home for commuters working in Bristol. There is no railway, but it is only a few miles from the M5.

Route: Wotton-under-Edge – Alderley – Hawkesbury Upton

Distance: About 7 miles

Map: O.S. Landranger 172

Start: The War Memorial in Wotton-under-Edge

Terrain: Quite demanding – no leisurely stroll, anyway. Level, steep, rough or muddy underfoot. A quagmire in places in wet weather. During a prolonged wet spell, wellington boots and a canoe are more appropriate.

Nearest Towns: Dursley, Stroud, Tetbury

Access: Depending on your approach, off the A46 or M5. There are many possibilities as shown on the map. Wotton is at approximate map ref: 760935.

Parking: There is a free car park at the start of Potters Pond in Wotton, but see below.

Public Transport: Linear walks are 'awkward' in the sense that one has to get back again. A bus is useful, or even essential. I have taken one from Yate to Wotton, walked the walk, and then taken another from Hawkesbury back to Yate. Planning and timing are essential. Including church browsing, the walk takes about three hours. Unfortunately, buses are not that frequent and times change. There are none at all on a Sunday. Best to ring Avon County County Council on 0272 290777. There is a railway station in nearby Yate.

Refreshments: Spoilt for choice in Wotton. Two excellent pubs in Hawkesbury – the Duke of Beaufort and Fox.

The Church of St Mary, Wotton

The Walk

The walk starts at the War Memorial. Go north-east, along Culverhay, past the presently pink Culverhay House to the thirteenth century Church of St Mary the Virgin. Through the churchyard – see the pinnacled tower – crocketed pinnacles – and go around to your right, to the south porch. Closing the first door . . . and how dark it seems . . . one's eyes take a few seconds to adjust. Inside, the font stands to your left. You will probably be surprised at the large number of tablets and monuments on the walls. Walking to the north side of the church and along the north aisle, you reach the small, attractive St Katherine Chapel; its old stone fireplace is now home to a less attractive radiator. Continue east to the tomb of Thomas Lord Berkeley (1417) and his wife, Margaret (1392). Their larger than life-sized brasses lie on top of the tomb. Brass-rubbers can use the two replicas resting against the north wall; after obtaining permission, of course. Walking south, a brass chandelier, dating from 1763, hangs above the choir. In the south-east corner stands the organ: 'THE GIFT OF HIS MOST SACRED MAJESTY KING GEORGE – 1726'. A history of the 'Schrieder' organ is on display: originally given to St Martin-in-the-Fields by George I, it was bought by Wotton's Reverend Tattersall for £200 in 1799, placed in a gallery at the west end of the church and moved to its present position in 1882. A full specification of the organ is also shown.

Return to the War Memorial – watch for traffic and take the first left, south-east, into Potters Pond. A few yards further, a free car park lies conveniently 'to foot'. Continue past the Ram Inn, through Sinwell and along into Coombe. Take care to keep left where the road narrows, ignoring the bridleway; the road descends to a green signpost. Bear right, joining the Cotswold Way.

One minute, smooth and mostly level – the next, a 20-minute uphill slog. This occurs several times during the walk, so be warned. From now on, keep a wary eye open for arrow-heads and white spots.

Climb the steep path to Lisleway Hill and continue left up Blackquarries Hill. Near the top, another signpost points right along a lane, stony but level, with dry-stone walling that has seen better days on either side.

Proceed to a gate and on – you will see Wotton laid out below – to a somewhat confusing post, an artist's nightmare – blue arrow, yellow arrow and the omnipresent white spot. Left, here, and around, above an amphitheatre – massively terraced and imposing. The woody views to south and west are magnificent. A short stepped ascent and then right, along to a clearing, where a Way post (which may be hidden by grass in the summer), leads away from the main path.

This secondary path descends through a hollow, which can present something of an obstacle course – often slippery and full of leaves and fallen branches. Over a stile and left to the road. Cross to another stile, where an arrow-head points to its bigger brother, stamped high on a telegraph pole, further along the field. Follow the faint outline of the path in the direction indicated – a succession of stiles, then up the gentle slope of Kennerwell Lane to the road junction.

Straight across, and you are in the village of Alderley, whose main claim to fame is that it was the birthplace of Matthew Hale, Lord Chief Justice of the King's Bench. By all accounts, a devout, kind and honest man, he was born in this Cotswold village in 1609. Such exceptional qualities in those times may seem something of a contradiction today, for he would not hesitate to condemn women to death for witchcraft! St Kenelm's Church is only slightly off the beaten track, and is worth a visit, if only to view from the outside. Apart from the tower, which is fifteenth century, the church was rebuilt in the early nineteenth century. Like several in the area, it is kept locked, though keys are obtainable. I wonder what the Lord Chief Justice would have thought had he been around today?

Continue through Alderley to the inevitable Way sign – left – a series of gates – a bridleway. Bear right and then left – a road, by which a stream runs, past Kilcott Mill and on to Lower Kilcott. A post points right up a steep hollow to a gate and along a field to the awesome Claypit Wood.

At the time of writing, the Cotswold Way has been resited, slightly. One used to take the left-hand stile and follow the white spots and yellow arrow-heads painted on trees at strategic points – arboreal orienteering. Now, there remains the bridleway, straight ahead. Awesome is probably a bit extreme: there is plenty of mud in wet weather; in the summer, a stick is useful to ward off brambles and nettles. Claypit Wood leads into

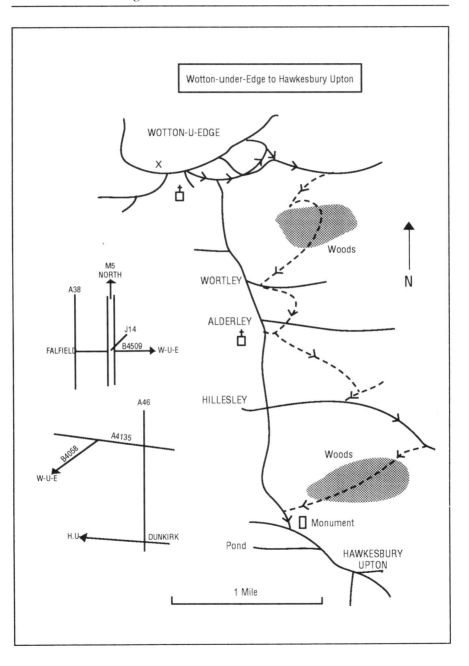

Wotton-under-Edge to Hawkesbury Upton

Frith Wood, which is easier. Beyond and across a field brings you to the main road.

Turn left, but please take care: it's a mite difficult to adjust to after footpaths. The pavement starts at the Somerset Monument which is closed – thank goodness – climbing steps to the top would really test one's stamina. Continue past the pond, and on into Hawkesbury Upton.

2. The Hawkesburys and Sodburys

The walk takes in Hawkesbury, Hawkesbury Upton, and three Sodburys – Chipping, Little and Old. The 'sod' of Sodbury is south, while 'bury' comes from the Saxon, meaning camp or fortification. Hence Sodbury – south camp – the name taken from the fort on Little Sodbury hill, which is crossed during the walk. Chipping was added to Sodbury when a market was established there in the reign of Henry III.

Route: Chipping Sodbury – Sodbury Common – Hawkesbury Upton – Hawkesbury – Little Sodbury – Old Sodbury – Sodbury Hill Fort – Old Sodbury – Chipping Sodbury

Distance: About 10 miles

Map: O.S. Landranger 172

Start: The War Memorial in Chipping Sodbury. Map ref: 728822

Terrain: A pot-pourri: long, level stretches of road; paths along fields that are sticky in places; several testing ascents.

Nearest Towns: Bristol, Bath

Access: The A432, which joins the A46 at map ref: 764812

Parking: There is a free car park in Chipping Sodbury

Public Transport: A regular bus service to and from Bristol. Best to ring Avon County Council on 0272 290777. There is a railway station in nearby Yate.

Refreshments: Plenty of pubs in Chipping Sodbury. The garage at Old Sodbury – more a motorists' takeaway, but useful.

The Walk

Start in Chipping Sodbury, by the War Memorial, turning left down Hatters Lane to a T-junction. Cross and take the first left over the cattle grid, along Sodbury Common, a reluctant host to the 'Travellers' in the

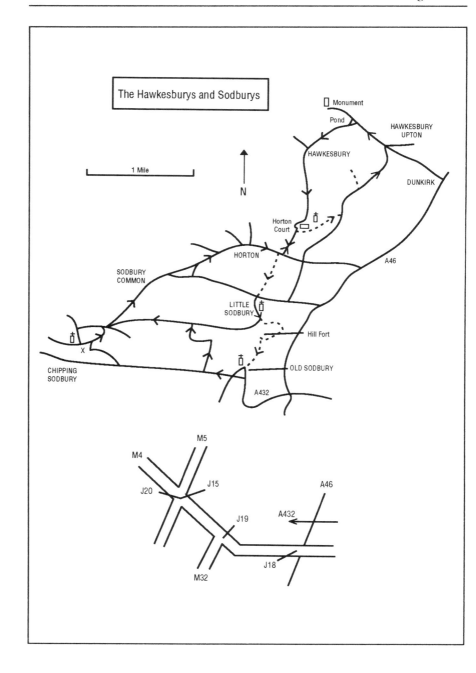

summer. Continue to the end of the common, over a second cattle grid and follow the road to Horton. A new village hall has been built, replacing the previous one which went up in flames. Sadly, the Post Office, tacked on to a bungalow, has gone. Village Post Offices are an endangered species. Walk up the hill through Horton and turn left at the school, joining the Cotswold Way in the process.

Follow the Way signs – a narrow stretch of road – and then right, over a stile, across a field – south-east – to a gate and another stile. You will see a yellow arrow-head on a post, one of several along this well-signposted section. The path ascends through woodland, around left, climbing steps, and levels – on to where an arrow-head on a tree points right to a stile. Leaving the trees, go through a gap in the hedge and across a patch of open ground. Beyond a derelict building, you come to a stile in the far corner. Up and over, and then right to Highfield Lane, leaving the Cotswold Way. Proceed left along the lane. The Way runs parallel for a while, but it can be very muddy walking and is best avoided. Straight ahead, on the horizon, the tip of the Somerset Monument is just visible. Continue past Highfield Farm where Highfield Lane becomes Sandpits Lane and enters Hawkesbury Upton.

Bear left, walking past the Duke of Beaufort to a pond, somewhat murky and drought-stricken, surrounded by a triangle of road. The Somerset Monument (forever closed for repairs, apparently) is five minutes away. Again, left here, taking the narrow road down a 1 in 7 gradient, past an old quarry, on into Hawkesbury.

The name Hawkesbury probably derived from Havoche's hill or camp, an early settlement in the area. Originally part of an estate of some importance, Hawkesbury is very quiet, little more than a scattering of farm buildings, a few houses, and a letter-box set in a wall. An indication of its former prominence is the exceedingly fine church of St Mary's.

The church is large and impressive, particularly the fourteenth century tower, adorned with battlements and gargoyles. Unfortunately, it is kept locked, but do take the time and trouble to obtain the key. Four options: the two nearest being Church Farm, opposite (the house with the letter-box), and The Old Vicarage at the back of the church. The porch is on your left, with a scraper on either side for muddy boots. Inside, St

Mary's is a mixture of the old and relatively new; it underwent extensive restoration in the late nineteenth century. As you enter, you will see a door to a Monk's room, hidden behind a curtain. A booklet may be purchased, and one may browse quite happily; though not for too long, there are still many miles to cover.

Leave the church (not forgetting to return the key) and continue through Hawkesbury, bearing left at the fork, signposted Horton. A walk of about a mile, passing Upper Chalkley Farm – beware: 'BULL BEEF – KEEP OUT' – approaching the fourteenth century Church of St James the Elder and Horton Court. The latter is run by the National Trust. Currently, the Norman Hall and Ambulatory are open to the public between April and October, on Wednesdays and Saturdays, from 2pm to 6pm. The Hall dates back to the twelfth century. The Court and Ambulatory were built in the sixteenth century for Dr William Knight who held high office under Henry VIII.

Around Horton Court the road is a mass of right angles. Negotiate and follow back to Horton (you've done most of this before, in reverse), and at the T-junction by the school, watch for the Way signs – right and then left – along a path between houses to a stile. Up and over, walking diagonally across the field. Down the grassy slope and up to a stile – there is a private lake on your left. Continue, crossing two fields and right over yet another stile, along a path which passes close by someone's back door, to the road. Here, lies Little Sodbury. Right, then left at the signpost.

On your left is St Adeline's church which, as the plaque in the church-yard reveals, was 'built in 1859 from the stones and plan of William Tyndall's little chapel behind Little Sodbury Manor'. The manor house is not included in the walk, being further on up the hill, behind the church. Tyndall lived there around the time of Henry VIII. He is known for his translation of the New Testament into English, most of this work being done abroad where he was finally charged with heresy and executed in 1536.

Proceed south, through Little Sodbury – the road ascends and, at the top of this modest climb, you will see the familiar Cotswold Way signpost. Leave the road and continue straight ahead to a gate where you turn left – a more demanding uphill section. Sharp right at the top, along to a stile and around to Sodbury Hill Fort.

Church of St Mary, Hawkesbury

An ancient construction, dating from the Iron Age, it has served both Romans and Danes. King Edward IV's army camped here *en route* to the Battle of Tewkesbury in the fifteenth century. Known locally as the Roman Camps, the fort measures approximately 300 by 200 yards, with double walls about 10 feet high, except on the west side, where a wooded slope falls away sharply. You can follow the Way straight across, but it is more interesting to walk around from the left on top of the inner wall.

Past the Roman Camps, you climb a stile and turn right down a hollow to a Way post which directs left across fields, eventually passing the primary school and reaching the road. This is Old Sodbury. Opposite, stands the Norman Church of St John the Baptist. A visit seems a good idea.

Pausing at the lychgate, one can read the names of the parishioners who gave their lives in the two World Wars. Inside, thirteenth century columns and arches run north and south of the nave. On your left, a choice of leaflets, Outlook (the Benefice Newsletter), and the fifteenth century font bring you to the west wall where are listed the names of past Vicars, from 1546 onwards. Walking along the north aisle, one comes to the north transept with its two effigies – one in wood, one in stone – and a piscina in the east wall. Beyond the pulpit, go into the chancel, and through the choir to the altar; the coloured tiles on the floor and the stained glass windows are particularly attractive. Return along the south aisle, past the nineteenth century organ in the south transept and back to the porch. Outside, go right to the wall, noting the battlemented tower with a pinnacle – crocketed – in each corner. There is a seat on which to rest weary legs (for a few minutes, only) and enjoy the view: green fields stretching to housing and the tower of the church at Chipping Sodbury (locked, unfortunately).

The Cotswold Way continues west; I prefer to return to the road, leaving the Way and bearing right, down Cotswold Lane to the A432. Again, right by the garage – it sells drinks and microwave snacks, if you are feeling peckish – walking along the pavement (Old Sodbury Post Office is still there) as far as the restaurant, La Capanna.

Right, here – arriving at a T-junction, you turn left, direction west, and follow the road along the edge of Sodbury Common, past Harwoodgate

Farm, to the first (and last) cattle grid near the start of the walk. Finally, cross the road and retrace your steps by way of Hatters Lane back to Chipping Sodbury.

Footnote: The walk traces a long figure of eight, and allowing for church browsing, takes around four hours. You can, of course, walk each section separately: starting at Chipping Sodbury, Horton, Hawkesbury Upton or virtually anywhere along the route. It is up to you.

3. Dursley to Hetty Pegler's Tump

The walk starts in the market town of Dursley — the car park off Hill Road, which lies alongside the Cotswold Way. It is, dare I say, quite demanding; crossing Cam Peak, Cam Long Down, and including a punishing ascent to the top of Crawley Hill.

Route: Dursley — Cam Peak — Cam Long Down — Hetty Pegler's Tump — Dursley

Distance: 5 to 7 miles

Map: O.S. Landranger 162

Start: see Parking

Terrain: Easy to difficult. Level to precipitous. Boots are recommended.

Nearest Towns: Stroud, Wotton-under-Edge

Access: The A4135 which passes through Dursley. Entering the town from the north-west, bear right at the lights, along May Lane, and then right into Hill Road. The crossing by the lights is littered with signs: if you should go left by mistake, follow the road around the Market House, going straight across, this time.

Parking: There is a free car park with public toilets off Hill Road. A 'maximum waiting 3 hours' sign is on the toilet wall.

Public Transport: The bus station lies alongside May Lane. Bus operators and times vary. Try Gloucester County Council on 0452 425543.

Refreshments: There is a café next to the bus station. It is closed on Sundays, but was also closed (permanently?) during a recent weekday visit, with rolls of carpets and furniture stacked inside. The Old Spot Inn, a Bass House, is next-door.

The Walk

From the car park off Hill Road, follow the Way into May Lane, past the bus station and library, and turn right into the pedestrian precinct, Parsonage Street. At the far end, you will come to the Market House: still used by street traders, it was built in 1738 and has a statue of Queen Anne on its east side.

Statue of Queen Anne, the Market House, Dursley

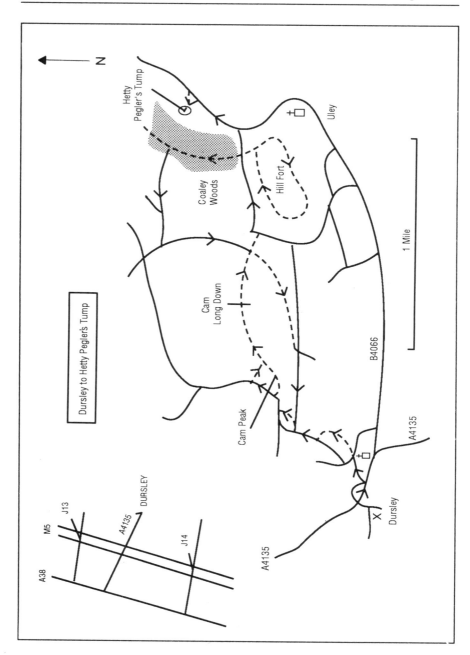

Continue past the Market House into Long Street. On your right is the Church of St James the Great. A visit before the walk seems in order.

Go through the churchyard and around to the right, the battlemented and pinnacled south side. The church has origins back in the thirteenth century and has undergone much alteration in the succeeding years. Inside, the font – fourteenth century on a modern base – stands to your left. In this south-west corner, pause and admire the two stained glass windows; they have a marvellous translucent quality, for me, anyway. In fact, there is much beautiful stained glass all around. Walking along the nave, into the chancel, past the choir-stalls: the east window, depicting 'The Ascension of our Lord', particularly catches the eye. There is a triple sedilia, with three cushions for the priests, in the south wall; and also a fine organ which dates from 1888. Returning along the south aisle, you will see a fifteenth century effigy lying on the sill of a window – all but the head, that is. Having summarised, I might add that a booklet may be purchased for fifty pence which gives a detailed history of the church. There are several free leaflets, too, describing the choir, the organ and the programme of Saturday concerts that are held throughout the year. To paraphrase: St James has a long tradition of music in the service of God.

Return to the road and continue right, down Long Street. At number 56, Raglan House, is a plaque commemorating the Danish inventor, Mikael Pedersen. He lived in Dursley at the end of the nineteenth century, and worked for Listers. Hardly a cause for celebration for walkers? Well, close enough; one of his inventions was a triangular bicycle with a string hammock saddle, which does sound rather painful. There used to be a Pedersen Cycles shop in Parsonage Street.

Bear right at the bottom of Long Street. Look for an arrow-head and white spot on a telegraph pole which directs you past the Lister bowling green, up a long flight of steps to a field. Follow the Way signs over a series of stiles – you can see Cam Peak in the distance. Finally, the path curves around to the left, and the road.

Right, here; further along you will pass Cam House School. In May, it boasts an avenue of pink-flowering horse chestnut. At the T-junction, take the stile, across a field of grazing horses, to Downhouse farm. Right, again, and then straight ahead, through the gate approaching Cam Peak.

Incredibly steep, the Peak is best climbed in zigzag fashion, and take care, for the grassy slope can be slippery when wet. There is an alternative easier route – the road around to the left, where a gate and path join the Way on the other side, approaching Cam Long Down. Worth trying the first time, perhaps?

The ascent of Cam Long Down is not quite so demanding, but rewarding in terms of the marvellous views over the River Severn and beyond – the Malverns can be seen on a clear day. Cam Long Down looks particularly good in May; covered, appropriately, with splashes of white may. Follow the Way signs, down steps, to a stile and the road. Continue past Springfield Farm where a post directs up a path leading to a hollow – muddy, even in dry weather. This stiff climb brings you to the top of Crawley Hill.

Take a well-earned break, and consider – there are two optional extras.

The first is to the right – a walk around Uley Hill Fort. Measuring in excess of thirty acres, it is ideally situated for defence. Many flint arrow-heads and Roman coins have been found. The walk affords views of Uley, Cam Peak and Cam Long Down.

Return to the road at the top of Crawley Hill and the second 'extra'. Turn left and proceed along the B4066 for about half a mile; take care as there is only a grass verge. You will come to a sign directing left across a field to Hetty Pegler's Tump. An unusual name – Hester and Henry Pegler owned the field in the seventeenth century – but hardly an impressive sight. The Tump is a neolithic long barrow where around twenty-eight people lie buried within a roofed chamber, 120 feet long. Beyond the entrance, which is only thirty inches square, is a gallery (crouching room only). Four sealed chambers – two on each side – lead off from the gallery.

Enough is enough: at Crawley Hill, continue north through Coaley Wood. Watch for the white spots. Mind where you walk, too; there are many trees down after winter gales. Further on through the wood, you come to the end of Knapp Lane. Leave the Way, here, bearing left, along this narrow, metalled lane with its attractive cottages on both sides. One such, has an old letter-box, painted blue, on an outside wall – not for general use. Turn sharp left at the junction by 'The White House'. This is easy, level walking back to the first farm beneath Cam Long Down, crossing your earlier route. Take the stile in the direction of the signpost which reads: 'Dursley 3Km'.

The path takes you across the edge of a field – weaving over and along a succession a stiles and railway sleepers – forever west – beyond a stone wall, to a lane. Bear left along this lane to a metalled road. Right, here, passing a Neighbourhood Watch Area sign to the T-junction, and then left, retracing your steps back to Dursley.

4. Triffids around Tormarton

The walk passes through Tormarton, West Littleton and Dyrham. Historically, three parishes lying in the hundred of Grumbald's Ash. Triffids abound, but more of them later.

Route: Tormarton – West Littleton – Dyrham Park – Tormarton

Distance: About 7 miles

Map: O.S. Landranger 172

Start: See Parking

Terrain: Mostly level, but exposed in places with sticky patches along fields in wet weather.

Nearest Towns: Chipping Sodbury, Bath

Access: See Parking

Parking: The lay-by off the M4-A46 interchange, junction 18. Map ref: 755778.

Public Transport: The occasional bus stops in Tormarton. Ring Avon County Council on 0272 290777.

Refreshments: Again, in the lay-by, but Monday to Friday only. For a lay-by, the facilities are quite good – tea, toilets, even a phone. A popular watering-hole for motorists.

The Walk

Parking in the lay-by near the M4-A46 interchange, junction 18, you follow the Way signs up a path, south-east, to the A46. Left here, walking along the grass verge. A white arrow-head on a post directs across the road to another lay-by. Cross with care and continue to the roundabout above the M4. Keep to the right, negotiating two slip roads to where a post points right along the A46; then right and right, again, opposite the entrance to Dodington Park. This single-track, metalled road leads to Tormarton.

You pass a white spot and arrow-head painted on a telegraph pole – at last – the green Cotswold Way signpost – left over a stile, across two fields to a gate. From here, you can see the top of the tower of Tormarton's church above the trees.

Climb the stile by the gate and proceed to the road, entering Tormarton. Secluded and quiet: Tormarton, like many a Cotswold village, has lost its Post Office and shops; yet new housing is going up all the time. The place grows despite having fewer facilities. Buses are a rarity. The answer, of course, is the car – essential for that trip to the shops, in Yate or Bath, perhaps. What will we do when the oil runs out? Go back to the horse-drawn Cotswold waggon and trundle along the (toll free?) motor-ways.

Church of St Mary, Tormarton

Turn left at the road, ignoring the Way post to Old Sodbury, crossing to the pavement opposite. Continue to where another Way post directs right; a new stile has been erected, here. Up and over, walking along pasture, nodding, in passing, to a couple of friendly horses (at the time of writing, anyway), to the road. Opposite, is the Church of St Mary Magdalene, which is well worth a visit.

Approach the church through an avenue of yews around four hundred years old. Gargoyles look down from the top of the tower. Originally Anglo-Saxon, the church was pulled down and rebuilt after the Norman conquest. There has been much restoration in later years. Internally, the font and pulpit are fine examples of the Norman and Jacobean styles, respectively. On the floor of the chancel (hidden under the carpet), is the outline of the figure of Sir John de la Rivere, a local benefactor; fourteenth century but in outline only, for the brass has gone. There is also a passage squint which leads to the south side, and further along, by the south wall, a fine brass to John Ceysill.

Leaving the church, turn left, along the pavement to the Portcullis. Cross and continue around to your left, signposted Marshfield, leaving the Cotswold Way. Further down, the pavement ends, so proceed along the grass verge, over a bridge spanning the M4, until you reach a T-junction sign and signpost – 'West Littleton 3km'.

Bear right, direction west, along what is really a bridleway – initially a metalled lane – to some farm buildings, passing Lower Lapdown Farm and a blue arrow-head on a post. The lane, grassy underfoot, opens onto a field and crosses to another. Here, cut diagonally along a narrow strip of grass, south-west, making for a pylon in the distance. At a gap in the hedge, cross the minor road with care. West Littleton is 1.5km away. You pass beneath a long line of electricity pylons – giant triffids – or their metal skeletons, trailing wire rope in their outstretched hands.

The land is exposed – high and arable – fields extend to every horizon. There always seems to be a tractor or two chugging away somewhere. The route widens, passes a barn and dips to the road, where you turn left, on to the village of West Littleton.

The road rises through the village. Go right, opposite the phone box, to the small nineteenth century Church of St James. Above, is a large bellcote – pyramid-shaped – a golden rooster surveys the scene below. Through the south porch, the font is on your left. High on the west wall is what appears to be a large brass, with red lettering: 'Glory to God in the Highest', dated 1856. A 'Cradle Roll' hangs on the north wall.

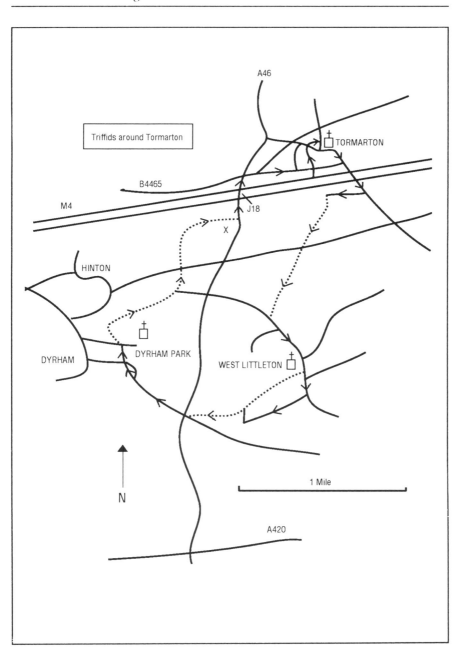

Back at the road, bear right – following it to just beyond the last house, where you turn right, direction south-west, along a lane. A feast of blackberries is there for the taking in the autumn. The lane is rutted and partly overgrown, but passable. Further on, go right, through a gate to where the lane ends. A yellow arrow-head on the fence points back to West Littleton. Its larger brother directs left – west – the gate is locked open. Take the latter – you will see a barn in the distance – and keeping the hedge to your left, walk along the field to a wooden gate which must be climbed. Over and around to the right of a barn, walking to an old stone stile and the road. Right, here, a matter of yards to the A46.

Traffic fairly zips along, so cross with care, taking the road opposite. On your right is Dyrham Park – you may see deer grazing. Continue down the road, passing a Cotswold Way sign to Bath and joining the Way in the process. It dips steeply – watch for the blind corners – you enter Dyrham village and come to a signpost set in a grassy triangle. Bear right, where further along, in passing, you will see Dyrham House and gardens. Public access is via the A46. Further along the road, another signpost – 'Tormarton 5km' – directs right up a steep path.

Follow the Way by the perimeter wall of Dyrham Park, noting to your left, below Hinton Hill, a stretch of strip lynchet terracing. Beyond, is a hill fort – the site of a battle between the Britons and Saxons in 577. The Saxons won, and the poor old Brits retreated to Wales and Cornwall to lick their wounds.

Turn left at the minor road and walk along to a T-junction where a signpost points across two fields (passing under those triffids, again). Finally, as ever, watching for the Way signs, bear right – a last field as far as a post – blue arrow-head and white spot – indicating the lay-by where the walk began and, possibly, a welcome cup of tea.

5. Painting Painswick

To do adequate justice to Painswick and its surrounds requires a much larger canvas than that covered by this article. A few brush strokes are all that I can manage; enough, I hope, to whet your appetite, for the walk is only part of the picture.

Route: Painswick – Pitchcombe – Painswick

Distance: About 5 miles

Map: O.S. Landranger 162

Start: See Parking

Terrain: Good, in general. Some gradients across the Painswick Valley. Sticky patches in wet weather, particularly around gates where cattle gather.

Nearest Towns: Stroud, Cheltenham, Gloucester

Access: M5, junction 13. Map ref: 778068. A419 to Stroud. A46 to Painswick.

Parking: The free car park off the A46: on your right as you appproach Painswick from the direction of Stroud. Map ref: 865096. There are toilets and a street map.

Public Transport: A few buses. Ring Gloucester County Council on 0452 425543.

Refreshments: Numerous pubs, the Falcon Inn, St Michael's Restaurant and Guest House (closed Mondays) in Victoria Street.

The Walk

First things first, however – let's stretch the legs. Leave the car park, turning right, walking up past the library (closed Wednesdays). Cross the road and proceed left along Edge Road, joining the Cotswold Way. You will come to a Way sign, and notice on a gate – 'Hambutts Field – property of The Open Spaces Society'. Left, here – the gate is easiest – along a field to a stile – the beginning of a narrow path between two garden hedges. Beyond, bear left, away from the road, coming even-

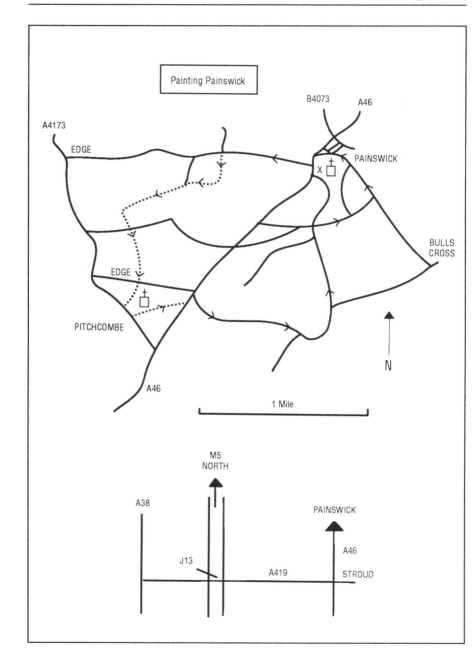

tually to another field. Directions are in the form of yellow arrow-heads and white spots, painted on trees. Continue, passing to the right of the tennis courts and on to a sort of giant white lollipop about one foot in diameter.

Take a bearing – direction west – and you will see a second lolly – off-white, this time, in the distance. Make for that – it is not as far as it looks – and a few yards beyond, where the path dips steeply into woodland, a stile. Over and along, through the gate by Washbrook Farm, turning left at the wooden signpost – 'Cotswold Way South – Edgemoor'. Walk up the path, close to two farm buildings and a rusting cement mixer, and then go left over a stile, passing a bench, courtesy of the Cotswold Voluntary Warden Service.

The path enters woodland – be careful, there are surface roots and it can be a mite slippery. A Way post directs down to a footbridge and up steps to a field. Bear left, towards the now-familiar arrow-head and spot on a tree, and on to a stile. Climb, and left, again, making for a narrow gap in the stone hedge and the road.

The Cotswold Way continues right, but you leave the Way, here, turning left, to an alternative signposted path (which can be hidden by foliage). Proceed as indicated – direction south. Now is a good time to stop and take in the fine views along Painswick Valley. The impressive spire of Painswick's church (more of that later) can be seen. With the hedge to your right, go through a second entrance, ignoring the track that bears right, keeping south, up and over a stile with staples in its step (useful when slippery). The tower of Pitchcombe's church should now be visible. Follow the arrow-head (slightly left) across the field to the corner of a wire fence, and on to a gate and lane which ends at the road. Cross and go left, a matter of yards to another gate, opposite a house called Halesmead. Squeeze through a gap near the gate and continue south, passing to the right of a line of fencing – descending and negotiating a muddy patch, then up to the churchyard and Church of St John the Baptist, Pitchcombe.

Inside, is a sketch of the church by M. A. Little, dated 1836. A larger picture hangs next to it – they seem different – a note explains why. The first church, a Norman saddleback, was built in the thirteenth century. A second one was erected in 1836, but burned down. The present church is about one hundred years old. According to the Vicar, the bell, 'Yohannes' by name, is fourteenth century – its rope lies conveniently to hand – temptation! Also, one may see a framed copy of the Table of Fees, dated 1872. Marriage by Banns – five shillings. Marriage by licence – ten shillings and six pence. The present fees are alongside – they seem quite reasonable, by comparison. Around to your left, in the north-west corner, is a stained glass window: imperfectly transparent, beautifully translucent – marvellous. Part of an early font is set in the south wall of the chancel.

Leave the church and go left through the churchyard, passing several table tombs and yews (a sample of the treat in store at Painswick), to a gate and the pavement. Left, here; a few yards further, beyond the bus stop, turn left along a tarmac drive. Keep to the left of the holly bush, leaving the drive, taking the path to a stile and field. This is rough pasture, which slopes, awkwardly. Walk down to the diagonally opposite corner, where a stile brings you to the busy A46.

Cross with care (traffic moves quickly) and proceed left along the pavement, then sharp right down Pincot Lane. This narrow, metalled lane meanders across Painswick Valley, ending at a T-junction. Left, here, as shown on the signpost – 'Painswick & Bulls X'. Thank goodness it does not read 'X Bulls', which walkers should, of course, avoid. The road takes you along the far side of the valley, passing Wells Farm and Juniper Cottages, and where it curves right – signposted 'Birdlip' – continue left – signposted 'Painswick' – down a one-in-eight gradient, approaching the outskirts of the town.

The route ascends, becoming Stepping Stone Lane. Turn right into Kingsmill Lane, beside a pillar-box set in a wall, walking past a mix of old and new houses. Several, to your right, are on quite a steep incline. Finally, you will come to a T-junction, where you bear left – a short, stiff climb up Tibbiwell Lane – then left again at The Cross (a name, only), into St Mary's Street. Ahead, are the churchyard and St Mary's Church, which really deserve an afternoon to themselves. But from the point of view of the walk, continue through the churchyard to the A46, then left, back to the car park.

Painswick, an old Cotswold wool town, lies in the hundred of Bisley. A true 'jewel of the Cotswolds'. It is interesting just to wander around the back streets, admiring the old stone buildings. The combined weight of the roof tiles does not bear thinking about.

Church of St Mary, Painswick

However, the church is Painswick's most outstanding feature. I would suggest that you first go to the church entrance – on your left as you enter the churchyard from St Mary's Street. Inside, you may purchase several leaflets at the very modest sum of twenty pence each. One is devoted to the church, itself – a guided tour, within. There are also two Tomb Trails, researched by Denzil Young, which are much more interesting than they sound. Have you ever experienced a 'stitch in the side' when walking? For fifteen pence, you can read about Embroidered Kneelers: nine categories – from Religious Symbols to Family Crests are covered.

All essential information is in the leaflets. I will note, only, that Painswick was originally called Wyke and had a church at least as far back as 1086 – Domesday Book records that Wyke had a priest, then. The church has a fifteenth century tower at its west end, topped by a spire. Lightning never strikes the same place twice, so they say – amend to twice in the same century; for the spire was hit in 1763 and again in 1883. Tower and spire are 174 feet high, overall.

Do take time for the guided tour inside the church. Also, do have a wander around the churchyard, using the Tomb Trails if you wish. There are (supposedly) ninety-nine mostly cone-shaped yews, about two hundred years old – a topiarist's dream, or nightmare? The tombs themselves are varied and interesting. I duly wandered and came across one – not a pedestal or table tomb – a slab in the grass. Henry Jordan, Yeoman, who died at the ripe old age of ninety-three.

The only problem with Painswick (to my mind), is the A46. Traffic is often heavy – single lane in one place, and one can clearly see how it is spoiling the town. Having said that, I have driven there many times (how else, on a Sunday); so what does one do? Build a bypass and destroy acres of beautiful countryside? I pass.

A day's outing is strongly recommended. All-round exercise – the body in the morning, pause for lunch – the mind in the afternoon. There's the countryside and a whole town to explore: church, churchyard, library, shops, back streets – a day is not enough, really. Now there's a thought – bed and breakfast is readily available.

A view along New Street, Painswick

6. Birdlip Walk

The walk starts in Birdlip, takes in Brimpsfield, Cowley, and for a grand finale, briefly touches the Cotswold Way at the Barrow Wake viewpoint. Pray for a clear day, for the views are magnificent.

Route: Birdlip – Brimpsfield – Cowley – Birdlip

Distance: About 7 miles

Map: O.S. Landranger 163

Start: See Parking

Terrain: Good, in general. One long and moderately steep gradient up South Hill. In wet weather, a sticky patch approaching Cuckoopen Barn Farm.

Nearest Towns: Stroud, Cheltenham, Gloucester.

Access: A419 or A46 to Stroud. B4070 to Birdlip. The B4070 from Stroud to Birdlip is an attractive ride.

Parking: Approaching Birdlip along the B4070, from the direction of Stroud – take care – Birdlip is a mass of confusing roads. Entering the village, turn right at the T-junction, and where the road bears round to the left, go straight across, passing Birdlip Stores on your right. Continue to where the road bears right (signposted Brimpsfield and Caudle Green), and again, go straight across to a bypassed section of the A417 – part of an old Roman road between Gloucester and Cirencester – noted Ermin Way on the map. Park the car anywhere beyond Birdlip County Primary School. Map ref: 930142.

Public Transport: A few buses. Ring Gloucester County Council on 0452 425543.

Refreshments: In Birdlip – the Royal George Hotel and Restaurant, Kingshead House Restaurant. There is also a Post Office-cum-general stores (open to 1300 Sundays) for nuts, fruit, chocolate etc.

The Walk

Leaving the car [see Parking], walk approximately east along the road, then take the signposted bridleway – right – through a gate, over a stile beside a double gate, across a field to the road. Left, here, finally negotiating three right angles (two are 'left angles'), passing the village hall and entering Brimpsfield. You will see a War Memorial on your right. Go straight across to the gate with the sign 'TO THE CHURCH', along a ribbon of concrete, by the remains of the once-formidable Brimpsfield Castle.

Church of St Michael, Brimpsfield

There is not much to see: traces of earthworks and a dry moat. The castle was built in the twelfth century for the Giffards. One such, John Giffard, an important baron of his time, made the fatal mistake of siding with Thomas, Earl of Lancaster in the barons wars. He was taken prisoner at the Battle of Boroughbridge and executed at Gloucester. A miffed Edward II sent soldiers to demolish his castle at Brimpsfield – which they did – comprehensively. Only the villagers gained – stones from the castle remains being used for their own houses.

Continue past the earthworks to a gate and grid and on through the churchyard, under three arches of yew to the south porch of the Church of St Michael. This is a beautiful little church, inside and out, that has a well used and cared for look about it. You may be lucky enough to obtain a booklet which contains a plan of the church: originally early Norman, parts date from the twelfth through to the fifteenth centuries. Inside, on your left, stands the fifteenth century font. There is a fine stained glass window with a marvellous pale, luminous quality in the west wall. Walking east, past the pulpit of carved oak, dated 1658, you come to a small chapel on the north side: '... created by the inspiration of the Rev. F. Eric Cottrell – a fitting memorial to his 15 years of work as a Rector of this parish.' In the bell chamber, a notice describes the six Brimpsfield Bells, and beyond, lie three medieval tombstones. The largest, which is quite massive, bears a sword carved in relief, and probably commemorates one of the Giffards.

Leaving the churchyard, turn right, direction north, walking across grass to a stile set in the stone hedge. Up and over to another stile and narrow road. Right, here – the road dips steeply, past Watercombe Farm, on up to the A417. There is plenty of traffic, so cross with care, taking the road through Cowley Wood. Emerging, and ignoring the first signposted footpath on your right that points south, you come to a white gate before some holly, and a stile. Climb and follow the faint path across the field (full of mole hills), north-east, making for Cowley Manor. Negotiate another gate and stile, and proceed left along the road to Cowley.

Cowley, a parish in the hundred of Rapsgate, is reputed to have got its name from a pasture where cows were kept, which does tie in rather neatly with its being the source of the 'milky' River Churn.

Turn right at the T-junction and on through the entrance of Cowley Manor, currently a Community Care Centre and Nursing Home run by Gloucestershire County Council. Make for a gap in the yew hedge to the Church of St Mary. Overshadowed somewhat by Cowley Manor, the church was built in the early thirteenth century, having undergone much renovation in succeeding years. Three of the six bells were donated by one Henry Bret, a squire of the manor in the eighteenth century. This

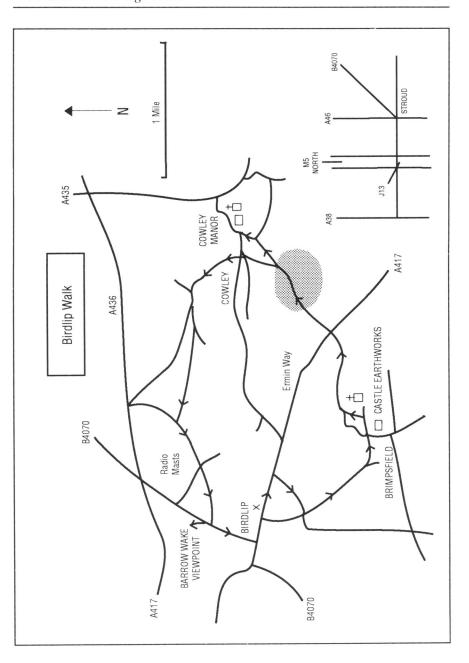

gentleman was passionately fond of bell-ringing. He used to travel the country with a company of bell-ringers – a Cook's tour for budding campanologists – managing to get through a large fortune in the process.

Retrace your steps back along the road, direction west, keeping straight on where it veers left, by a sign on the wall which reads: 'Manor Barn B & B', and then a few yards further, bear sharp right up a hill. A long stretch of narrow road that eventually curves left and passes another road on your right. A matter of yards to a signposted 'public path' – go left here. There are marvellous views all around as you begin the long climb up South Hill – a prelude to the often-crowded Barrow Wake. Avoid the gate on your left beside two blue arrow-heads on a post (an alternative route). The path levels out – a gate – a stile and across a field, which can be very sticky in wet weather. Be warned: the heavy clay clings to your boots and slowly builds up. A decoke is often necessary.

Finally, you reach the oddly-named Cuckoopen Barn Farm. A notice on a post at the entrance to the farm commemorates the building of the world's largest straw rick – 40,400 bales! Continue along what is now an unsurfaced lane, bearing left at the 'T-junction', south-west, passing Rushwood Kennels and the radio masts. Straight ahead, around and down, under the A417; then right, to the Barrow Wake viewpoint.

A popular place with motorists. On a clear day, there are superb views towards Gloucester and beyond. There is an excellent panoramic topo-graph and an interesting geological topograph – five hundred million years of history – in memory of the geologist P.J. Hopkins. There is also a plate describing the Cotswold Scarp and the discovery of the Birdlip Mirror.

Walk south, towards Birdlip, back along the edge of the road that leads from the viewpoint. A pavement begins – cross – entering the village – then left, returning to the start of the walk.

7. Around Kingscote

The walk traces a rough figure of eight, passing through Kingscote and Newington Bagpath. There is also a more demanding optional extra, a trek through Kingscote Wood. Please see the footnote near the end of this article. It starts in the spacious car park at the back of the Hunters Hall Inn [see Access]. Temptation ... you might even arrive during a car boot sale, held occasionally on Sunday mornings.

Route: Kingscote – Horsley – Kingscote – Newington Bagpath – Kingscote

Distance: 3 or 7 miles

Map: O.S. Landranger 162

Start: See Parking

Terrain: Varied. Plenty of level road walking, but several steep sections and the difficult Kingscote Wood.

Nearest Towns: Dursley, Stroud, Tetbury

Access: A46 to the junction with the A4135 at Calcot Farm. Map ref: 838950. Then along the A4135 towards Dursley. The Hunters Hall Inn is on your left.

Parking: The car park at the back of the Hunters Hall Inn. Map ref: 814960

Public Transport: A few buses, privately operated. No Sunday service. There is a bus stop opposite the Hunters Hall Inn. Ring Gloucester County Council on 0452 425543.

Refreshments: The Hunters Hall Inn. AA 2-star and Egon Ronay Recommended. Food, drink, hotel and conference suite.

The Walk

Park the car and cross to the road opposite, making for Kingscote. Entering the village, follow the road around to the right – signposted Hazlecote – on past the church, which we will look at later, and continue as far as the village hall.

Left, here – direction north, and you are soon on high, exposed ground –

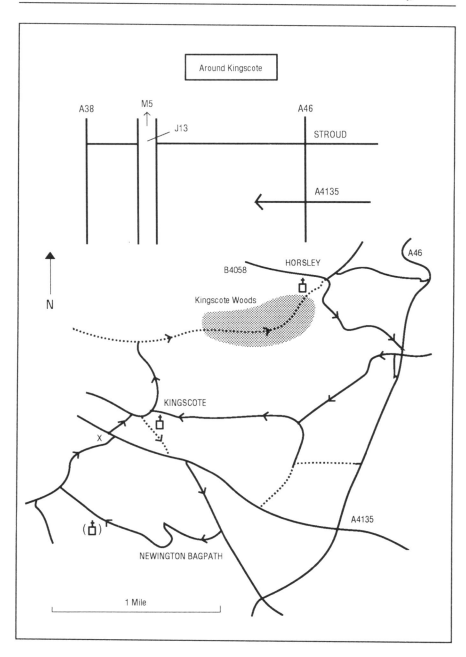

certainly not the place to get caught without a waterproof. Continue past a cluster of farm buildings, down towards, but not as far as, Binley Farm. You will see a large house to your right. Leave the main track here, taking the right fork, and just before a pond and willow inside the house grounds, bear right, east, along a path. Pass through the gate and follow the main path for about thirty yards, then fork left, down to another gate – the entrance to Kingscote Wood.

The path is narrow at first, and can be extremely muddy in places. It is possible to avoid the worst bits by plunging into the undergrowth to left and right (an exaggeration, maybe, it depends on the time of year). Through the gate at the end of the wood and the walking is easier, more woodland on either side, approaching the outskirts of Horsley.

Beyond the first few houses, bear sharp right, taking the road to the oddly named Tiltups End. The last time I walked this section, dry-stone walling was going up on my left – a really professional job. Continue down past Lower Hay Farm, with its tennis courts, and then make the steep climb up to the A46. Tipputs (not Tiltups) Inn is on one side. Do not cross, but go right, around the garage, and then sharp right in a westerly direction. Proceed along this narrow road to a T-junction. An Ordnance Survey Triangulation Station is set in the wall, opposite. Again, right here, and back, finally, to Kingscote.

Kingscote – King's Wood – lies in the hundred of Berkeley. Tradition has it that there was once a city in the area. The remains of camps, buildings and many Roman coins have been found. A Roman coffin was discovered in the churchyard, while ploughing in 1872. Parts of the Church of St John date from around the thirteenth century. The church was extensively restored in the nineteenth century. In the north porch is recorded the marriage of Edward Jenner (the pioneer of vaccination) to Catharine Kingscote on 6th March, 1788. Inside, it is rather dark – light switches are to your right. In the north-west corner is an extract from the will of one John Wight, dated 1838: ' ...leaving to the minister of the church £100 in trust to invest in funds of Great Britain and to divide and distribute the dividends.' Quite a sum in those days. There are several tablets and inscriptions on the walls: walking east, one such records a tribute to Joe Anthony Francis Parkinson: '... who fell at Bethune, France on 13th Oct 1914.' On through the chancel arch, the nineteenth century stained glass catches the eye.

An equine view at Newington Bagpath, near Kingscote

Church of St John, Kingscote

Leaving the church (not forgetting to turn off the lights), go around to your right, passing the monuments and table tombs to the Kingscote family, to a gate on the opposite side of the churchyard. Walking in a southerly direction, along a grassy path across a field, it ends in a strip of concrete and gate, which opens onto the A4135. Turn left along the grass verge and cross (watch for traffic), taking the minor road a few yards further on your right, south-east; and then another, again right, by some farm buildings, signposted Newington. Follow the road down – it winds, and ascends steeply, up to the former church of St Bartholomew, Newington Bagpath.

A sign of the times: I say 'former', because the church was declared redundant and closed for worship in 1975. St Bartholomew's has been sold, though at the time of writing, much conversion work still needs to be done before it can be made habitable. Private residence or derelict – visit and you will see. Currently, it is possible to walk around (but not inside) the 'church', and visit the graves which are kept separate and were not included in the sale.

Continue up and along the road to a T-junction and bear right, signposted Kingscote and Tetbury. You will eventually pass Bumpers Island Farm and Bumpers Isle Farm (B & B sign). A contradiction, really, and I cannot resist it: walking Bumper to Bumper. This is the final stretch – up and around a blind corner (take care), back to the start of the walk. Feel free to purchase a car boot if you wish.

Footnote: as stated previously, the walk traces a rough figure of eight – three walks for the price of one. An easier alternative, therefore, is to walk the second part – Kingscote and around Newington Bagpath – a distance of about 3 miles, avoiding muddy Kingscote Wood. If you decide to tackle the wood, please do wear boots rather than shoes – the going is not only muddy in places but rough underfoot, as well. It's worth the effort, though, as the woodland views are magnificent, particularly in spring and autumn.

8. A Daglingworth and Two Duntisbournes

The walk traces a very uneven figure of eight through Middle Duntisbourne, Duntisbourne Rouse, Daglingworth and Bagendon – all lying within the Hundred of Crowthorne and Minety (really, part of the Cirencester Hundred). Intriguing names, often with origins that go back to Saxon times.

Route: Perrott's Brook – Middle Duntisbourne – Daglingworth – Bagendon – Perrott's Brook

Distance: Up to 7 miles

Map: O.S. Landranger 163

Start: See Parking

Terrain: Mostly level. The occasional sticky patch.

Nearest Towns: Cirencester, Cheltenham, Gloucester.

Access: A choice of A417, A419, A429, A433, A435 towards Cirencester. Perrott's Brook lies along the Cirencester – Cheltenham stretch of the A435.

Parking: The car park beside the Bear Inn at Perrott's Brook. Map ref: 019059

Public Transport: Ring Gloucester County Council on 0452 425543.

Refreshments: The Bear Inn. Weather permitting, why not relax with a drink in the garden?

The Walk

There is a car park at the Bear Inn, conveniently alongside the A435, at Perrott's Brook. Begin by taking the road to your right as you face the inn, walking in a westerly direction. Straight on at the crossroads a few yards ahead. The road ascends, past Lyncroft Farm, along to Bagendon Downs Farm, where you take the right fork, signposted Birdlip and Gloucester. In a garden on your left stands a young *Araucaria*, the monkey-puzzle tree, covered in a cobweb of what looks like clematis – a striking combination in the sun in late spring.

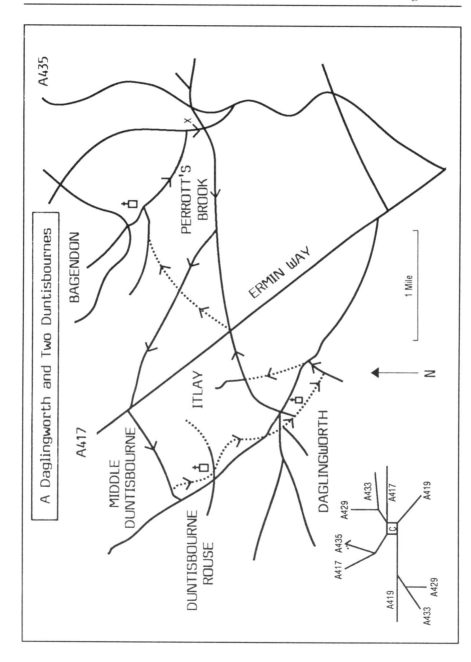

A Daglingworth and Two Duntisbournes

Walk the level stretch of narrow road to the A417, site of the old Roman Road from Cirencester to Gloucester, marked Ermin Way on the map. Traffic is heavy, so cross with care to the road opposite. Further on, you pass the house of Edward Martin who makes and sells replica staddle stones, once used to keep mice and rats out of corn ricks. Nowadays, they make an attractive garden feature – you will see many examples of his work in the neighbourhood.

Continue, entering Middle Duntisbourne; go over the stream and then left, off the road, through a gap between a house and barn – a yellow arrow-head directs. Then up the grassy slope, veering left, south-east, to the corner of a wall. Another arrow-head is painted on a stone in the wall. Follow the path down and along by the stream, over a stile, eventually reaching St Michael's Church, Duntisbourne Rouse.

Church of St Michael, Duntisbourne Rouse

Of possible Saxon origins, the church appears marvellously compact and solid with a squat saddleback tower at its west end. It has much to offer. The decorated font is thirteenth century. Walking east towards the chancel, note the foot-operated organ on one side (read the sisterly inscription), the Jacobean pulpit on the other. The wall painting running (not walking) along the entire length of the north chancel wall is fifteenth century. The small stained glass window in the east wall catches the light beautifully. On a more mundane note: it is interesting to look through the visitors' book – there are entries by people from South Africa and New Zealand, and even far away Cheltenham. One gentleman comments that it took three attempts to find the place.

Leaving the church, proceed south-east down the churchyard, through a gate, along the path, down steps to the road. Left, here, over the stream (again), past Woodside Cottage to where a sign directs right – Grove Hill and Daglingworth.

The path snakes across the field, through a gate, along the edge of two fields (which can be muddy), eventually joining the road into Daglingworth – a name derived from the Saxon, meaning 'Hidden Village'.

Bear right at the junction, and a few yards further on, left, over a stile, walking past back gardens, down steps to the road. Cross to more steps – ascend and negotiate an odd combination of gate and stile, a field, two more stiles, and then turn right, approaching the Church of the Holy Rood, Daglingworth.

A trifle dark inside? The notice above a shelf on your left gives the location of the light switches. There are also several leaflets which describe the church in some detail. It has many Saxon and Norman features – a prolonged browse is recommended. I will just add that the tower is fifteenth century and the church underwent major reconstruction during the mid-nineteenth century.

Leave the church and go left, south-east, taking the signposted bridleway to Lower End. A gate, a field, another gate and around to your left, past Daglingworth Manor to the T-junction by Hawthorn Cottage. Bear left a few yards, and at Little Garth, take the path opposite that passes to the left of The Old School, direction north. Arriving at the cross-roads – Italy is opposite – turn right, towards the A417.

Cross this busy road and continue through the gate that stands on the left-hand corner of the Perrott's Brook road – '1989' is scratched in the cement on top of the wall. Walk north-east, to another gate and another field – and there's the quarry – lots of lovely Cotswold stone. In dry weather, lots of Cotswold dust, too, so be warned. The gate at the end of the field opens to the road. There is a lane opposite – level though sometimes sticky, it soon descends, ending at a narrow road, where you bear right, entering Bagendon. Unfortunately, St Margaret's Church is kept locked, but it is worth the walk just for the view from the road and perhaps a stroll around the churchyard.

Leaving the churchyard, turn left, direction east, veering south-east: easy, level walking to the junction; then turn right, signposted Perrott's Brook and Cirencester, back to the crossroads near the start of the walk, and the Bear Inn.

Footnote: discouraged by May's long, wet grass, you may prefer a slightly shorter option: the road back to Perrott's Brook at the junction before the quarry – map ref: 001056 – avoiding Bagendon. Another, is to park opposite Daglingworth Church and walk the second part of the figure of eight, taking in the two Duntisbournes. Sundays excepted: this space is really only for church parking.

9. Ozleworth

Ozleworth — Ozla's worth — lies in the Hundred of Berkeley. The parish is thinly populated — one of its attractions, really. On the other hand, this does present problems, for by no stretch of the imagination can Ozleworth be described as easily accessible [see Roads]. However, it is worth the effort; you will amply rewarded with a visit to a very fine church, almost unique in its way, and a walk through a National Trust Park, containing much woodland and wildlife.

Route: Ozleworth — Newark Park — Ozleworth

Distance: A modest 4 miles

Map: O.S. Landranger 162

Start: See Parking

Terrain: A pot-pourri of muddy paths and muddy roads, especially in winter. Boots are recommended. A long climb through Newark Park.

Nearest Towns: Dursley, Wotton-under-Edge, Stroud, Tetbury.

Access: A46 to the junction with the A4135 at Calcot Farm. Map ref: 838950. Then along the A4135 towards Dursley, taking the road left to Ozleworth (which is signposted) at map ref: 792964. Finally, left again, through the entrance of Ozleworth Park.

Parking: The parking space beside Ozleworth Church. Map ref: 795934

Public Transport: None

Refreshments: Take a flask

The Walk

The walk starts alongside the Norman Church of St Nicholas, in Ozleworth Park. There is ample space for parking in front of the church. Having parked, you will no doubt be keen to get walking, but who can resist at least a preliminary inspection?

The Church of St Nicholas has been placed in the care of the Redundant Churches Fund. A 'retirement home' for churches, typically those in

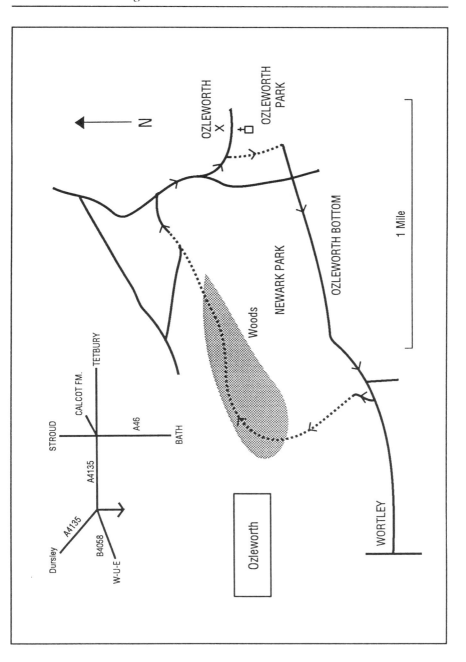

areas of declining population, no longer used for worship, which are, nonetheless, considered worth preserving.

Unusually, the churchyard is circular, surrounded by a dry-stone wall. Walk around to your left – the porch is on the opposite side. The oldest parts of the church – tower and chancel – were most probably built by Roger de Berkeley at the beginning of the twelfth century. The rarest feature is the central tower, an irregular hexagon. There is also a decorated font which is thirteenth century. The church has been altered and added to many times in subsequent centuries. Two prominent families – the Clutterbuck's of Newark Park and the Rolt's (Sir John was MP for South Gloucestershire) – are commemorated in the beautiful stained glass windows.

The Church of St Nichlolas, Ozzleworth

Now for some exercise: leave the churchyard and bear left, walking to a point just beyond Ozleworth Park House. At the railing fence, take the path sharp left, due south. Continue down to where it veers left, but go straight on, through a gate and around to the right, up towards a house, two gates and the road.

Straight across, here, along Ozleworth Bottom, in the direction of Wortley. The road is narrow and although metalled, can be very muddy. The trees on either side tend to form a canopy overhead – it is almost jungle-like. At the risk of being alarmist, you may pass a 'Beware of the Bull' notice on a gate – which is open, and the same sign a little further on – gate closed. No sight of the bull in either case – at least, not when I was there.

Continue to the entrance of Newark Park. This is National Trust property – over 600 acres of wooded and agricultural land, much of which is private, though there is a public right of way. Turn sharp right, walking past Lower Lodge and around to a gate. Follow the bridleway signs. The path ascends, steeply at first, easing to a more gentle climb. The views are impressive, particularly during spring and autumn. Even the massive root systems of trees downed by the winters' gales catch the eye. You come to another gate that has an awkward, spring-backed bolt. Further along, take the narrow path that forks left, by a wall, and then bear right, approaching the entrance 'proper' of Newark Park House.

For a paltry pound, you may visit the house – it is open to the public during the months of April, May, August and September. Wednesday and Thursday afternoons.

At the entrance, proceed left, along the metalled lane, direction northeast, past Lion Lodge, to the road. Right, here (but not right, again, as indicated by the footpath sign) – you will see a triangular 'gates' sign a little further on.

The good news is that the rest of the walk is nearly all downhill. Continue past Fernley Farm, straight on at the crossroads, to the junction. There is a letter-box on one side, a telephone box on the other (marked on the map). Turn right (you probably drove along here, earlier), taking the road down to Ozleworth Park, and then bear left, through the park entrance, back to the start of the walk.

Roads: a note of warning regarding the road off the A4135, to Ozleworth: not only is it narrow – in winter, one would have to redefine the words 'mud on road'. While the lane through Ozleworth Park is 'rough' in the extreme. Don't bother to wash your car before your journey.

10. Tetbury and Shipton Moyne

Tetbury is a thriving market town of considerable character and charm, with a recorded history stretching back beyond its dominance as a wool town to the existence of a Saxon monastery in the seventh century. Earlier still, there is evidence of Roman occupation – it was even settled in pre-historic times. The church, of course, dominates; its tower and spire can be seen from miles around. We will visit St Mary's at the end of the walk – the icing on the cake.

Route: Tetbury – Shipton Moyne – Tetbury

Distance: About 6 miles

Map: O.S. Landranger 173

Start: See Parking

Terrain: Mostly level, but sticky in places.

Nearest Towns: Malmesbury, Cirencester, Gloucester.

Access: A46 and then A433 or A4135. The A433 from the direction of Cirencester. The B4014 from Malmesbury. Tetbury is at approximate map ref: 890930.

Parking: A confusing selection. I have assumed that you are approaching Tetbury from the south-west, along the A433, through Didmarton, past the entrance of the Westonbirt Arboretum, through Doughton and then over Bath Bridge into the town. Ascending beyond the bridge, you will see a car park sign on your left at the entrance to Old Brewery Lane. In fact, there are several along this lane; free parking presents no problem. There is a toilet – a sort of DIY lavatorial space module – cost 10p.

Public Transport: Ring Gloucester County Council on 0452 425543.

Refreshments: Spoilt for choice in Tetbury.

The Walk

First, the walk – leave the car park in Old Brewery Lane [see Parking], cross to the pavement opposite and bear right, down Bath Road. As you start to cross Bath Bridge, look down to your left – see the rabbit topiary? Beyond the bridge, where the pavement ends, you will come to the Old Toll House. There is a circular plaque on the wall, commemorating Tetbury's 1300 years of recorded history. Ignore the first signposted footpath on your left and continue along the grass verge to another, close to the sign noting the twinning of Tetbury with Zwingenberg.

Left, here; as an additional reference, the name Starveall is on a garage wall. Follow the path between two hedges – dry and clear in cold January – full of long, wet grass on a rainy day in May – to a gate. Continue around to the left, direction south-east veering south, and keeping the hedge to your left, cross several fields, through a gap in the fence to a patch of rough, open ground. Still with the hedge to your left, but moving away from it slightly (the ground becomes very soggy further on), go through a new wooden gate and follow the path along by the stream. Walking south-west, you come to another gate with a yellow arrow-head on a post and a final gate which must be climbed. Ignore the first crossing over the stream, taking the wooden footbridge a few yards further. Ascending, you then go along the edge of a field to a long, low farm building. Right, here, taking the lane to a house and the road. Turn left, a long stretch of road, that enters Shipton Moyne.

The origin of Shipton is none too clear: possibly from the fact that sheep were kept here, or from a past owner of the town. Moyne was certainly taken from the family of Le Moygn, who owned the manor of that name.

Bear left, just beyond the Cat and Custard Pot Inn (now there's a name!) along to the Church of St John the Baptist. Although mostly rebuilt in 1864, St John's has origins back in Norman times. Inside, the name Estcourt figures prominently; in fact, generations of Estcourts are commemorated. There is an Estcourt Chapel and a large tomb with effigies of Thomas Estcourt (1599), his wife and family. The church also has many beautiful stained glass windows.

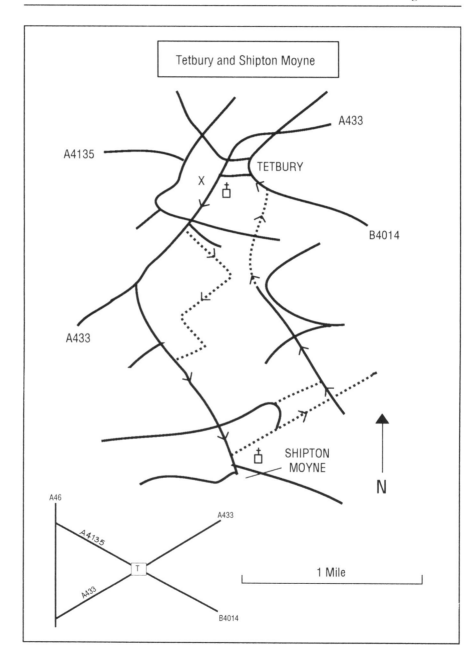

Leaving the church, bear right through the churchyard, roughly east, following the path over a stile, ignoring the surfaced lane to your left – straight on, through an awkward double gate, to an often muddy lane. Do not continue across the field, opposite, but bear left, approaching Manor Farm. Another double gate – the lane acquires a welcome concrete surface. Cross the cattle-grid and on towards Estcourt House. Beyond, take the right fork, direction north, and where the lane curves north-west, continue across the grass – still north – to a barbed-wire fence. Fortunately, a section of the wire is sheathed in wood and painted a light blue (visible from the lane). Over and along, you will see a white disc on a tree trunk – make first for that and then another, a bit further on. Continue down to a stile, and an arrow-head directs you to a wooden footbridge. Follow the path around to the right, passing beside the remains of an old stone stile and over a small stone bridge, and then round to the left. Here, one can go north-west a few yards to a gate and complete a circle, but the ground is very 'pondish', even in the summer, and is best avoided. A drier option is to keep to the path, climbing steps to a gate.

Left, here, north-west, coming eventually to the lane that leads to Slads Farm. Go straight across, taking the stile, then head north. Several fields and stone stiles later, with the tower and spire of Tetbury's church looming ever larger, pass through a gap in the fence to a lane and the B4014, the Malmesbury road. Cross to the slightly wider pavement opposite, and walk along Silver Street, up into Tetbury. Bear left into Barton Abbotts, and just before The Rectory, take the entrance into the churchyard. The right-hand path leads to the church entrance.

I will not attempt a detailed description of the Church of St Mary. You may buy several leaflets for only a few pence which do the job much better than I. However, to whet your appetite: walking around the outside, pinnacles, tower and spire particularly catch the eye. The church is medieval in origin; tower and spire, rebuilt in 1891, reach to 186 feet. There are ambulatories around most of the church. Four stone effigies are sited in the north passage. Walking east along the nave: two brass chandeliers, dated 1781, hang above you and box pews line both sides. Look back and see the organ in the gallery and then forward to the enormous stained glass window behind the altar. St Mary's really demands a good hour of your time.

Leaving the church, go west along the stone path, under an arch, to the road. Old Brewery Lane and its car parks are nearly opposite.

The Market House, Tetbury

11. Leighterton and Beverston

The walk offers a look around two churches, passes the ruins of a castle and affords views of the Westonbirt Arboretum. Please do wear boots, particularly during the winter months, as use is made of several bridleways (a horse is optional).

Leighterton lies in the Hundred of Grumbald's Ash. Its roots are in agriculture. However, this changed temporarily with the advent of the Industrial Revolution, when nailmaking predominated, but by the end of the nineteenth century Leighterton had returned to the land.

Route: Leighterton – Beverston – Westonbirt Arboretum – Leighterton

Distance: 6 or 8 miles

Map: O.S. Landranger 162

Start: See *Parking*

Terrain: Mostly level, but mucky in places.

Nearest Towns: Wotton-under-Edge, Stroud, Tetbury, Bath.

Access: Any of several roads off the A46. There is one at map ref: 810906. Leighterton is at map ref: 824910.

Parking: In Leighterton, but not ideal. There are a few side-roads. I prefer to park alongside the wall opposite the church. Incidentally, there is a car park behind the Royal Oak, which I have used – but only once. The landlord was 'politely stroppy', insisting that I ask his permission in future (problems with lorries parking overnight). Would he appreciate an early morning call on a Sunday?

Public Transport: There is a bus stop and shelter in Leighterton, but woefully few buses. Best to ring Gloucester County Council on 0452 425543.

Refreshments: The Royal Oak.

The Walk

Whether parked down a side-road or by the wall [see Parking], make for the Church of St Andrew. The church dates from the thirteenth century and was extensively restored in the nineteenth century. Enter via the south porch, heeding the notice and closing the first door (to keep out the birds). Inside, on your left, is the fourteenth century decorated font. The tower has a timber-framed belfry and a carillon of eight tubular bells – 'Harringtons patent tubular bells, Coventry', to be exact. Sheet music by numbers. Walking east, in the chancel there is a thirteenth century piscina and three attractive lancet windows: 'Erected in loving memory of John Leigh Reed by his wife and children'.

Leaving the church, bear right at the road. Go right again, at the T-junction, signposted Westonbirt and Tetbury, passing the Post Office and ignoring the footpath by Holly Tree House, which is something of an obstacle course. I made one attempt – ploughed fields and a fence – fixed, deliberately, I fear, in front of a stile. The road curves sharply to the left, past Bennett's Farm – a long, narrow stretch to the crossroads.

Here, take the road opposite, signposted Tetbury, and proceed to the Hookshouse Pottery: 'Handthrown garden ware and domestic pots'. There is a showroom where one can browse, perhaps even buy something? But not too big, for there is much walking to do.

A few yards beyond the pottery, turn left along the unsurfaced lane, direction north, through a gate which asks to be kept shut but which is often tied open. You will see a blue arrow-head on a post. The lane opens onto a field – keep to the right where it forks, still approximately north, walking along by a railing fence to another gate. The lane narrows somewhat – grass and a sprinkling of nettles – eventually reaching a section of dry-stone walling with a neat curve to it. Go straight ahead, north-east, along the bridleway. Another blue arrow-head directs. The spire of Tetbury's church pierces the right horizon. You come to a large, new double gate and the busy A4135, the Tetbury road. Cross with care and walk left, along the high grass verge. An awkward couple of minutes, marred slightly by the oncoming traffic. Entering Beverston, slowing at the 40 mph sign, the grass verge gives way to a welcome pavement.

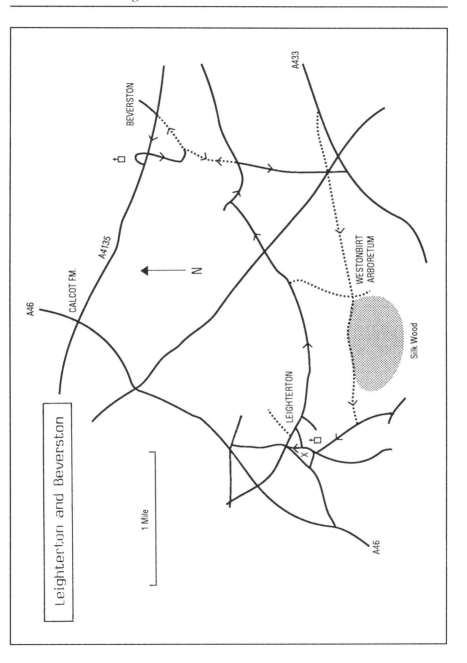

Leighterton and Beverston

BEVERSTON

A433

WESTONBIRT ARBORETUM

Silk Wood

LEIGHTERTON

A46

CALCOT FM.

A4135

A46

N

1 Mile

Continue as far as the enticing sign – 'To the Norman Church'. Who can resist? Right, here, around the back of Beverston Castle. A peek over the wall reveals the castle wall and traces of a moat. With origins in Saxon times, the present remains are thirteenth century. The castle was repaired and added to in succeeding centuries, notably by the Berkeleys. Built square with a tower at each corner, it is an impressive reminder of times past.

Follow the lane around to the right – and there stands St Mary's Church. The church has undergone many alterations over the years; not least, an extensive restoration in the nineteenth century by the architect, Lewis Vulliamy. The battlemented tower has a pinnacle at each corner. Hardly part of the architecture, but just inside is an old stove that is kept stoked in the winter months – most welcome to cold weather walkers. Along the nave stand two columns and three pointed arches of distinction, which are thirteenth century. There is a brass on the north wall to Roger O'Gorman, and another, just above it, to James Garlick. The Berkeley Chapel is in the north transept; from there, you can walk through a squint passage (mind your head) to the chancel. Here, you will see a fourteenth century piscina in the south-east corner and a brass to Jacob Hayward in the chancel floor.

Leave the church and turn left, past the entrance to Beverston Castle, which unfortunately is not open to the public. At the road, go straight across, by the 'no access for lorries' sign. Beyond Park Farm, the tarmac surface gives way to grass, leading you down to what can be a very muddy and wet stretch – the lane acts almost as a drain. Approaching that curved dry-stone walling, retrace your steps to the Hookshouse Pottery.

At the pottery, take the Westonbirt road – south – another long, narrow stretch, past Field Barn Farm, to the crossroads. Opposite lies a signposted footpath – over the stile, walking west, across a field, keeping the hedge to your right. This can be quite sticky underfoot. Continue through a gate. A wall to your left, marks the start of the Westonbirt Arboretum – with free 'arboreal' views. Cross several fields and then go down a hollow, which veers right, around to gate – the beginning of a wooded section. A bridleway, really – muddy, too; chopped up by horses' hooves.

Beverston Castle

Having emerged relatively unscathed from the trees, now is a good time to have a 'decoke', getting all that mud off your boots – it really clings, doesn't it? There are plenty of sticks around. Further on – a choice: gate and bridleway, or stile and path. I prefer the former, but do watch where you walk – the surface is rutted and full of tufts of grass.

Eventually, you come to the road. Turn right, walking the final stretch to the crossroads at Leighterton. Right, again, past the pond, where the pavement begins, and back to the start of the walk.

Footnote: in outline, the walk is a squashed rectangle with a Y-shaped Beverston optional extra tacked on at the top. This adds an extra two miles, which includes an awkward couple of minutes along a high grass verge and a stretch down a wet and muddy lane. However, I think it is worth the trouble – St Mary's at Beverston should not be missed.

12. Driffield and The Ampneys

The area is rich in history. It is kind to the walker, too; reasonably level with many quiet, narrow roads and signposted footpaths through the glorious Gloucestershire countryside. I 'did' this walk in the spring and still remember frisky black and white lambs, pink and white flowering cherries – and churches; this part of the county has more than its fair share of churches. The walk includes three, and also a hill fort as an optional extra.

First a note on pronunciation – when saying 'Ampney', omit the letter 'p'; you are a native, at least for a day.

Route: Ampney Crucis – Driffield – Ranbury Ring – Ampney St Mary – Ampney Crucis

Distance: About 5 miles

Map: O.S. Landranger 163

Start: See *Parking*

Terrain: Mostly level. Sticky across fields in wet weather.

Nearest Towns: Cirencester, Cheltenham, Gloucester, Stroud, Tetbury, Malmesbury, Fairford.

Access: From Cirencester, the A417 in the direction of Fairford.

Parking: In the lay-by along the half circle of road at map ref: 073017. To get there, take the first left, about a quarter of a mile beyond The Crown of Crucis in Ampney Crucis. The village itself is two miles from Cirencester on the A417, the Cirencester to Fairford road.

Public Transport: Ring Gloucester County Council on 0452 425543.

Refreshments: The Crown of Crucis at Ampney Crucis. AA 3 star – hotel, restaurant and bar.

The Walk

And so on to the walk. Having parked [see Parking], proceed west, bearing right just before the bridge over Ampney Brook. Beyond Ampney Brook House, take the path to your left which opens onto a field. Continue straight ahead, ignoring the right fork. The farmer has thoughtfully left the path alone, but it can be a shade sticky underfoot in wet weather. You will see a small cricket pavilion in the distance. Continue past the trough (water for animals only), over two stiles, to the road.

Left, here, and then first right, just before the War Memorial. There is some attractive dry-stone walling on your right. Further along, you will come to the Church of Holy Cross, Ampney Crucis. The cross itself is early fifteenth century and stands to your left as you walk through the churchyard. One cautionary note – the church is locked at night. Enquiries revealed that 'it is opened first thing in the morning.' I have been disappointed once, only; so don't get there too early. Inside, the church is impressive; examples of Saxon through to nineteenth century architecture may be seen. The tower and sanctus bellcote are fifteenth century. Browse and you will see remains of fourteenth century wall paintings, the tomb of George Lloyd and his wife with the figures of their twelve children on the sides, and a preacher's hour glass on the pulpit. Uniquely, in the south transept, are the Pleydell tablets recording the day and hour of death of members of the Pleydell family.

Retrace your steps to the road by the memorial and bear right, over the bridge, to the A417. On your left is the Crown of Crucis [see Refreshments]. Cross with care, taking the Driffield road, south. Towards the end of April, the trimmed hedges are beginning to 'green up'; in a few weeks they will 'mushroom' and the road seem twice as narrow as before. This longish stretch curves round finally to a staggered crossroads – right a few yards and then straight across, through Harnhill, towards Driffield. Further on, you will see the small tower of Driffield's Church of St Mary.

Medieval in origin, the church looks its best from the outside. The tower is eighteenth century. Internally, it has been restored twice: in 1734 and 1863; it is mostly nineteenth century, now. There are wall panels showing The Lord's Prayer and The Ten Commandments.

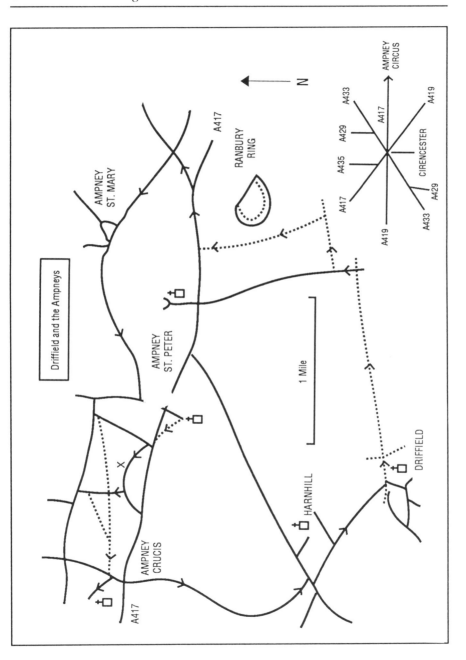

Returning to the road, turn right and immediately right again. With the farm to your left, pass through two gates (the ground can be very muddy, here) to a field. Take the path approximately east. At the far corner, you cross a footbridge and are presented with three choices: straight ahead by the hedge (north); right towards some trees; or the central path, direction east-north-east. Take the middle road, more an unsurfaced lane, across the field, over the stream to just beyond a house and outbuilding. A short strip of concrete – and then left along the metalled lane for about fifty yards, where you turn right, walking as far as the end of the left-hand hedge. A small building is shown on the map but is no more. Left, here, keeping the hedge to your right, making for the distant trees.

This is the optional extra that I mentioned earlier – bear right through the gate alongside the trees – a rough, wooded tract – a walk of around ten minutes to the Ranbury Camp or Ring. An Iron Age hill fort; hardly a ring, being somewhat irregular in shape. The area defended is about twenty acres. It is possible to walk part of the way round. Part has been fenced off.

Back at the gate, continue north, past a water tank, down to the A417. Cross to the pavement opposite and proceed right, as far as the Red Lion, where you take the left fork, signposted Ampney St Mary. Further along, bear left, walking through the village and beyond, past Forty Farm – a long stretch to the T-junction. Turn left, here, and continue down, inevitably, to the A417.

The best has been kept to the last. Cross the dual carriageway to the Church of Ampney St Mary. Oddly, it lies about a mile from the village; due, it is believed, to the ravages of the Black Death in the fourteenth century. Walking through the churchyard you will see a cross carved out of a tree, and behind that, on the north wall of the church, above a blocked doorway, an early Norman tympanum. The carving represents the Lion of Righteousness overcoming two agents of the Devil and a griffin – powerful stuff. The church entrance is at the back. Inside, is a sheer delight. The cracked paving on the floor; the parish chest with 1725 etched on one side, and three locks, requiring the presence of the rector and two church wardens before it could be opened; the hat pegs along the walls; and most interesting of all – the scraps of medieval wall paintings.

Tympanum, Chuch of St Mary, Ampney St Mary

This twelfth century church is known locally as the ivy church. Three guesses? Well, it lay in disuse for over thirty years, and before its restoration in 1913, fell prey to Hedera Helix. Put another way – acquired an ivy overcoat. Truly, a treat that should not be missed.

Leave the church by a different route – the path south, bearing right, over a wooden bridge to a field. Right, again, walking beside Ampney Brook until you reach a gate – permanently open, locked in brambles – to the A417. Turn right along the grass verge for a few yards and cross to the house opposite (Stonelea), and then left, into the half circle of road, back to the start of the walk.

13. Bisley

The walk starts in Bisley, a large Cotswold village of narrow streets, packed tight with centuries-old cottages and houses. It then circles around Througham and Througham Slad, passing close to Lower Battlescombe and the elusive Giant's Stone.

Route: Bisley — Througham — Througham Slad — Battlescombe — Bisley

Distance: Up to 5 miles

Map: O.S. Landranger 163

Start: See *Parking*

Terrain: Mostly level with some rough and sticky patches.

Nearest Towns: Stroud, Cirencester, Tetbury.

Access: Entering Stroud along the A46 from the direction of Bath — just beyond the 'Stroud' sign, at the first roundabout, take the A419 Cirencester road. Bisley is well-signposted from then on, the first turning being to your left. Bisley is at approximate map ref: 905060.

Parking: Approaching Bisley, one has the choice of bypassing or going through the village. Choose the latter, down to the T-junction — opposite is George Stores. Left, here, then right, immediately opposite The Stirrup Cup — a 'no through road'. Take care, as there are roads everywhere. A few yards further on is a sports ground and car park.

Public Transport: Ring Gloucester County Council on 0452 425543.

Refreshments: The Stirrup Cup.

The Walk

First, an important preliminary: leaving the car park, turn right, walking down to the Stirrup Cup. Left, here, along the High Street, past George Stores – and take care, for there is no pavement in places. Continue past Swiss Cottage (far from London), the Old Post Office, the Court House, and then right, up Church Hill, mounting steps through the lychgate to the Church of All Saints, Bisley.

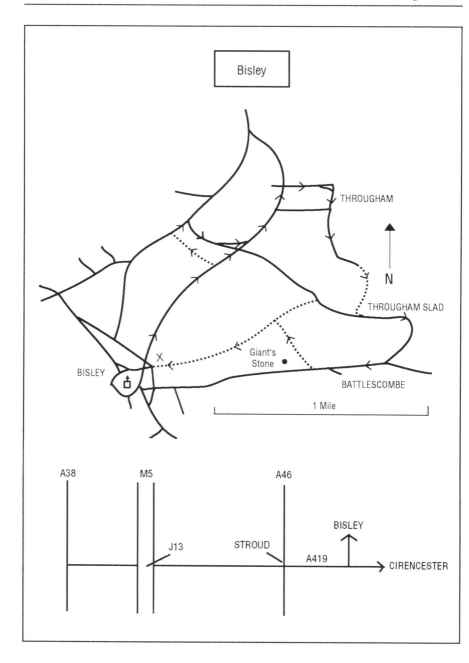

Of thirteenth and fourteenth century origins and restored in 1862, All Saints is a fine church with many interesting features, and well worth a visit. The entrance is on your left, the south porch. Beyond, still in the churchyard, stands a thirteenth century well head which once held a poor souls' light, around which masses were said for the poor. Inside, a modern touch, the All Saints Bisley Lending Library – three shelves of religious works. A booklet may be purchased for forty pence. Walking to your right, along the south side towards the Lypiatt Chapel, is a small brass, no more than eighteen inches high, to Kateryn Sewell. Below, and even smaller, are what one might call two 'mini-brasses' of her seven sons and five daughters. In the Lypiatt Chapel is the thirteenth century effigy of a knight, lying with legs crossed, feet resting on his favourite dog. The stained glass windows in the chancel and the choir-stalls whose candlesticks and candles are currently embellished with flowers are both very pleasing to the eye. Beside the front pew on the north side is a framed brass rubbing. Finally, return along the north aisle, around past the richly decorated Norman bowl of the font to the south porch.

High Street, Bisley

Retrace your steps back to the Stirrup Cup, taking the road signed 'Unsuitable for heavy goods and wide vehicles', walking north-north-east, past Fir Tree Cottages, the Priest's Barn and a windpump.

Further on, where the road curves left and dips – an optional extra which avoids the valley climb yet is quite difficult. The path is marked on the map but has an abandoned look about it. Turn left, just before a telegraph pole, passing to the right of a barn, on through a gate which is not easily opened, to two more gates standing side by side. Choose the right-hand one, painted a dark green. Continue across the field, keeping the hedge to your left, to a rickety gate which 'opens' onto a patch of rough ground, heavily overgrown. Take out the machete and cross to another gate, equally rickety – difficult to open – a wobbly climb. One more field and a farmyard bring you to the road. Bear right along the grass verge, and right, again, at the junction, signposted Througham. Keep left where the road forks, walking east, veering north-east, joining the main route, which is as follows:

The main and easier route follows the narrow road as it descends and ascends through the valley; finally ascending very steeply. Continue straight ahead at the minor crossroad, direction north-east, veering north – a long, level stretch, making for the rectangle of road that surrounds Througham.

Take the second turning right (which is unsigned), passing beneath a high stone wall crammed full of ivy. Bearing right is the order of the day: on past The Old Picture House, a letter-box, and a magnolia (stunning in March and April). Walk south, to where the road rises slightly and curves to the west, completing the rectangle. Here, go straight ahead, leaving the road for an unsurfaced lane. Take care, for the lane is rough underfoot and can be muddy in places. It serves as a bridleway and is wide enough to accommodate farm vehicles. Go past an old stone building, squeezing by a gate and another gate, the lane narrows and descends to Througham Slad.

Fend off several over-friendly dogs and continue down, past a fading yellow arrow-head on a post, a barn and stables. The lane curves right – a large house stands to your left – a backcloth of green rises to the east – on over a stream, and up to a gate beside a cattle grid, joining another lane, equally rough underfoot. Right, here, past the entrance to Lower

Battlescombe, walking north-west for about two hundred yards to a point just beyond a couple of posts, one on either side of the lane. To your left you will see a gas cylinder; to your right, a path. The gate has a spring-backed bolt and is tied with string – climbing is easier. According to the map, The Giant's Stone – one of the stones that formed the chambers of the Giant's Stone Barrow – lies nearby. One may walk around the mound – overgrown and a victim of dumping, but will be hard-pressed to find the stone – removed, buried or hidden among brambles.

You come to a smaller gate which opens onto a field. Bear left, north-west, and Derryards Farm is on the horizon. Keeping the hedge to your left – two gates in close succession – walking west – you can see a barn in the distance with the tip of the spire of Bisley's church poking above; it is almost as though the spire is part of the barn. Finally, navigate a stile that rocks dangerously (or go through the gate), walking past the barn, which has a ventilating tunnel temptingly deep within, back to the start of the walk.

14. Splatt Bridge to Saul Junction

This is a walk through a different part of Gloucestershire. There are few hills to climb and wooded valleys to admire, but the area is attractive and interesting, in its own way. For example, you will visit two fine churches and stroll alongside part of the Gloucester and Sharpness canal.

Route: Church End – Gloucester & Sharpness Canal – Wheatenhurst Weir – Church End

Distance: About 5 miles

Map: O.S. Landranger 162

Start: See *Parking*

Terrain: Level with some sticky patches across fields in wet weather.

Nearest Towns: Dursley, Gloucester, Stroud.

Access: At junction 13 of the M5, take the A419 and the B4071 to Frampton on Severn, and then left, to Church End.

Parking: There is a small car park opposite the Church of St Mary in Frampton on Severn.

Public Transport: Ring Gloucester County Council on 0452 425543.

Refreshments: The Three Horseshoes Inn.

The Gloucester and Sharpness canal was surveyed from Gloucester to Berkeley by R. Mylne in 1793. Unfortunately, it fell victim to financial problems which delayed its construction and also resulted in it terminating at Sharpness. With much celebration, the canal was finally opened in 1827. Trade has changed with the years – timber, grain, salt and oil, but the introduction of motor transport has led to a decline in recent times. Who knows? Fuel is becoming increasingly expensive – perhaps this more leisurely means of transporting goods from A to B will come into its own again. There is even talk of moving water along canals to relieve the effects of drought in some parts of the country.

Canal view, Frampton on Severn

Here endeth the preamble (or 'preramble') to the walk which starts in the small car park opposite the Church of St Mary in Frampton on Severn. The church should not be missed – its tower, topped by gargoyles and pinnacles can be seen for miles around. If locked, a notice in the porch advises: the key may be obtained at Church End House – the tall house on the corner with a green door.

Leaflets are usually available giving a history of the church, but I will summarise, just in case. St Mary's was consecrated as a parish church in 1315 and twice restored in the nineteenth century. Inside, on your left, is an ancient Romanesque lead font. Walking east, you will see two effigies in recesses along the wall of the north aisle: a knight holding a shield – he is believed to be a member of the Clifford family; and a Lady, probably also a Clifford. Beyond, in the chancel, hangs a chandelier – look up and you can read the inscription: "THE GIFT OF MRS. ELIZ. WINCHCOMBE. 1756". Beneath the east window – The Last Supper and many old tiles, some behind a curtain; feel their rough surface. Also, on the south side, a triple sedilia and piscina.

The Walk

So, at last, to the walk, itself. Leave the church and bear right, direction west, past the car park, to a stile. A yellow arrow-head points right, but go left, along the path, through an open gate, approaching the Gloucester and Sharpness Canal. Follow the path beside the canal as far as Splatt Bridge. A notice on the bridge warns – 'speed limit 6 mph' – applying to boats, not walkers, I think. Cross and then go immediately right, through a white gate, before walking north along the path on the far side. Looking back, there are impressive views across the canal – excellent for photography and painting (water-colours, of course). There is also much wildlife, even a heron or two. House-boats are often moored along here; some have intriguing names.

This is a long, level stretch to Fretherne Bridge, where you cross the road (not the bridge), go through a gate and continue straight ahead, making for Sandfield Bridge. See the canal lights? Again, straight across – the path widens and brings you finally to Saul Junction, a meeting of the waters.

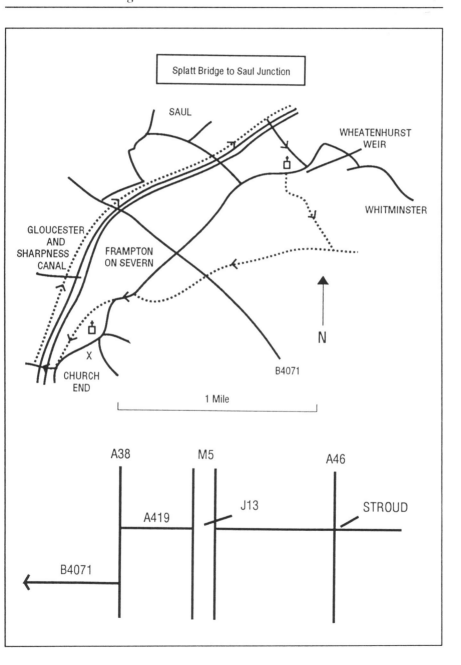

Splatt Bridge to Saul Junction

Cross the footbridge over the canal and then turn immediately left, in front of Junction Bridge House. Continue for a few yards and bear right, through a gate, over two stiles, walking roughly south-east, towards St Andrew's Church, Whitminster. You can see the church tower in the distance. At the far end of the field, another gate and small bridge to two more gates. Take the right hand one – beside a yellow arrow-head and spot on a post, walking up a grassy lane, passing the grounds of Whitminster House, where a peacock usually presides. The churchyard lies opposite.

In the churchyard, take the steps on your right that lead to Whitminster House. It is here that you may, if you wish, obtain the church key. A quite massive implement, which fits the lock of the side entrance in the west wall of the church. There is a leaflet inside St Andrew's which may be purchased for a few pence, and which gives a short history and description of the church.

Leave the churchyard, walking south, through the wrought iron gate and along the lane – where it curves left, continue straight ahead to the road. Turn right along the road, ignoring the signposted path to Whitminster. It is best to cross for there is a blind corner and the road is narrow. But it is only a matter of yards, past the letter-box and Bherunda, to the bridge over the River Frome at Wheatenhurst Weir.

Beyond the bridge, take the signposted footpath left, over a stile, walking by the impressive looking (and sounding) weir to two gates. Climb the stile beside the gate to your left, next to the sign 'Frampton and District Angling Club' and follow the path to another stile – a high one. You will see a small concrete bridge on your left.

The route from here to the road is somewhat tortuous. Bear right, west – a footpath across a field, and then through an open gate which has seen better days, but which still has a fading arrow-head on a post as a guide. Along another field, walking roughly north-west – you will see the handrail of a footbridge in the distance. Cross, following the line of the bridge, keeping the hedge to your left. Where the field ends, go straight on past a rough patch of ground to the corner. Follow the hedge – a succession of right angles – always with the hedge to your left – coming at last to a gap in the hedge. Walk west across a field which opens onto a grassy path and comes, finally, to the main road, the B4071.

Opposite lies the entrance to Frampton Court. Beyond the small gate on the left stands a post with a large yellow arrow-head. Take a bearing – north-west – ideally keeping a respectable distance from the water. There are lots of ducks about and it is rather mucky underfoot. You are making for a spot just to the left of some cottages – a good ten minutes' walk – to a wooden fence and stile. Careful, the stile is wobbly. Right, here, passing Fitcherbury East and Fitcherbury to the road. Then left, near several lovely old thatched cottages, crossing to the Three Horse-shoes Inn and down The Street as far as the telephone box. Go through the lychgate, walking south-west along an avenue of trees, back to St Mary's. One more 'up and over' – the very first and last stile – to the start of the walk.

15. Strolling Slad

The walk traces a rough circle around Slad, a Cotswold village that has not really taken to the motor-car. Parking, one might even say, is difficult. The alternative, a bus from nearby Stroud, is possible – but only just; buses are few and far between. Optimistically, I have assumed that you are parked at the beginning of Steanbridge Lane [see Parking and Public Transport].

Route: Circular route around Slad

Distance: A modest 4 miles

Map: O.S. Landranger 162

Start: See *Parking*

Terrain: One steep section. In wet weather, a generous helping of mud, and long, soaking grass across fields.

Nearest Towns: Gloucester, Stroud

Access: From Stroud, the B4070 – an attractive ride. Slad is at map ref: 872074.

Parking: Limited parking is available at the entrance to Steanbridge Lane, which is on your right as you pass through Slad from the direction of Stroud.

Public Transport: A few buses. Ring Gloucester County Council on 0452 425543.

Refreshments: The Woolpack and its Cider with Rosie bar, the other enduring feature of the village (see church detail). Naturally enough, there is no mention of this in the church leaflet.

The Walk

First, a short detour – proceed left along the pavement beside the B4070 – a walk of about three minutes, down to the Church of the Holy Trinity. The entrance is on the west side. The church was built in the 1830s by Charles Baker of Painswick. Inside, a free leaflet is available, written by the Reverend Barry Coker. Times change, as the vicar says in the leaflet: 'Over the years the village has lost its School, its Shop, its Post Office and its Vicarage – but the Church remains.' Another brief quote: '... a simple village Church ...', which describes it exactly – modest, neat and functional – open to visitors and used for regular worship, which is something, nowadays. A visitors' book is there for the signing, while contributions to the Slad Church Restoration Fund are much appreciated.

Return to Steanbridge Lane and continue beyond Catswood House, around to the right and down, past the tennis courts, negotiating the blind corner with care, for the road is narrow. A few yards further, take the path, right, before a large pond-cum-small lake, direction south-east. At the stile (one of many), you will see the familiar yellow arrow-head on a post. Over and on, up a field full of nettles and thistles, keeping the hedge to your right. In the top right-hand corner, another stile, following the path under low branches to a third stile. Often, the ground is quite muddy on the other side, but it is possible to make a slight detour around to the left. Continue south-east, with the hedge to your left this time. Look to your right and there is Slad laid out below – the church with its small spire, a string of houses and the surrounding woodland. Sometimes cattle graze in this field. I had the mildly disturbing experience of being followed by a herd of them. Heavy, bovine breathing – I felt like John Wayne in reverse.

Proceed through an old orchard to two gates, tied in various ways with binder twine. After a struggle, I untied and tied, managing a couple of reef-knots (not grannies). John Wayne would have coped superbly, I suppose. On past Furners Farm, around to the left and where the stone wall ends, take the path to your right – it is not signposted but clearly visible. Prepare for a shock at the next stile – it has an electric fence warning notice stuck on top (take care, anyway). Walking due west, cross a stile and then a wooden footbridge. Note the direction of the arrow-head – south-west. Half-way across this field, you will see two gates, one may be open – make for the gate to your left. Of course, it has a stile beside it, and another of sorts a few yards beyond. Hardly a stile; basically, some wood strung between two posts. A line of telegraph poles crosses the next field – aim for the pole that has a row of shiny green insulators on the top. A final stile brings you to a lane. Turn left, here, along to the road.

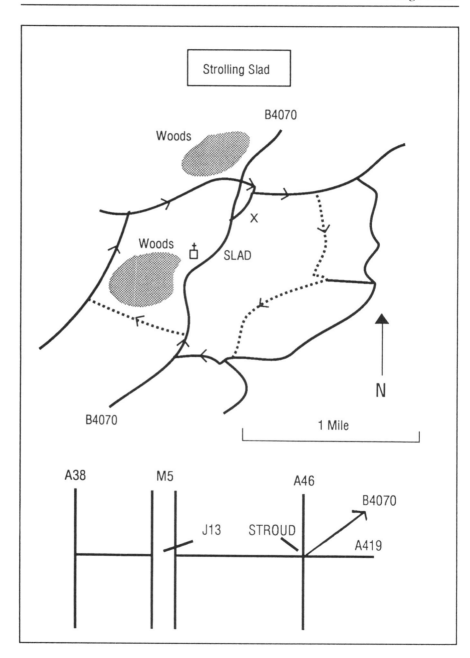

Church of the Holy Trinity, Slad

Bear right at the road; in fact, right is the order of the day: winding, descending, and ascending to the B4070. And right, again – a pavement, at last -approximately fifty yards beyond Woodside House, look carefully at the opposite side and you should see the sign: 'Woodside Bungalow' lying in the hedge. Cross with care and take the narrow path, north-west, that starts by the end of a wall.

This is the only really demanding ascent of the walk. Initially, the path is very steep. It passes a green letter-box and arrow-head on a post, then eases and widens to a rough, unsurfaced lane and gate. Continue along the edge of a field, by a drinking trough (murky water), eventually passing Folly Acres which, according to the notice, is 'a rural conservation and organic growing study centre'.

The ascent ends at the road. Turn right, walking approximately north, past Worgan's Farm Cottage, outbuildings and a last barn, currently packed with bales of hay. Bear right at the T-junction, south-east, descending, finally, to the B4070. The Old Vicarage is on your left.

Cross to the road opposite. There is a seat beside the War Memorial if you want to rest the legs and take in the view. The very narrow road descends and curves sharply to the right, where you join Steanbridge Lane and retrace your steps back to the start of the walk.

16. Purton, Slimbridge and Sharpness

This is, for the most part, a linear walk – two-way linear – there and back again: from Purton to Shepherd's Patch, beside part of the Gloucester and Sharpness canal; a small circle around Slimbridge which includes a look at a fine, old church and then back to Purton. There is also an optional extra – Purton to Sharpness.

Route: Purton – Shepherd's Patch – Slimbridge – Purton – Sharpness

Distance: About 8 miles. The Sharpness section adds another 4 miles

Map: O.S. Landranger 162

Start: See *Parking*

Terrain: Level with sticky patches across fields in wet weather.

Nearest Towns: Dursley, Gloucester, Stroud

Access: Taking the A38, from Bristol to Gloucester, turn left just before Berkeley Road. Purton is well-signposted. Smile, for you will pass through Halmore, the village of the candid camera.

Parking: There is a free car park at Purton – on your right as you enter the village.

Public Transport: None that I could see. Try Gloucester County Council on 0452 425543.

Refreshments: Two pubs at Purton. The Berkeley Hunt Inn lies near Purton Lower. There are public toilets on one side. Further down the road that leads towards the River Severn is the Berkeley Arms, an old-fashioned pub with loads of atmosphere.

I attempted a brief history of the canal in the walk 'Splatt Bridge to Saul Junction'; merely to add that it is just over 16 miles long and that today's main 'commodity' is leisure: fishing and dare I say, walking? Boat trips in the summer are popular, too.

This is easy, level walking – easy on the eye. The rippling water, colourful house-boats and varied wild life make this a very pleasant walk, indeed. Getting there without a car is difficult. I have assumed that you are in the car park at Purton and cannot resist a quick look at Purton's Church of St John the Evangelist. Not particularly steeped in history, but clean and tidy, and used for regular Sunday worship. At the time of writing, the organ, built by Lyddiatt & Sons and installed around 1906, is in dire need of overhaul and repair. A copy of an estimate lies on a table inside the church. Subtle hint, for a fund has started – feel free.

Canal view, Purton

The Walk

Leaving the church, make for the bridge, opposite. There are two swing-bridges over the canal at Purton – both automatic. Stand well clear when the red lights flash and the bell rings, for a boat is coming. The operation is quite interesting to watch. Cross Purton Upper and turn right along the canal path – direction south, veering east.

From observation, I would say that fishing is a predominantly male pursuit, though I can't say why. I'm told it's a good way of relaxing – switching off. At weekends, in particular, the banks are lined with fishermen. Nowadays, fishing requires more than a stick, piece of string, hook and worm. The 'gear' is formidable. Rods long enough for feather-weight pole-vaulters to use, trays of bait including writhing grubs that make one's stomach turn, keepnets and even a catapult or two. Then, of course, there's a seat, waterproofs, a thermos, some sandwiches and so on.

Boats of all shapes and sizes navigate up and down the canal. Look for the stubby house-boats, smartly painted, chugging along. Less attractive are the World War II pill-boxes that may be seen between the canal and the River Severn.

This section of the walk takes about fifty minutes and brings you to Shepherd's Patch. Here, cross Patch – hand-cranked, this time. On your left is the opportunity for a quick cuppa [see Refreshments]. Having crossed and possibly supped, continue down the road, direction south-east, past the Tudor Arms, making for Slimbridge. Take care, for the road is narrow and can be busy in the summer (the Wildfowl Trust is nearby). You should be able to see the spire of Slimbridge's church in the distance.

Where the road starts to curve left, just beyond the house, Kingston, turn right along Lightenbrook Lane. Fifty yards further on, to your left, is a signposted footpath, a walker etched in wood. Go through the gate and across the field, due east and over stiles, along a path full of brambles and nettles, to the road and Slimbridge. The Post Office is opposite.

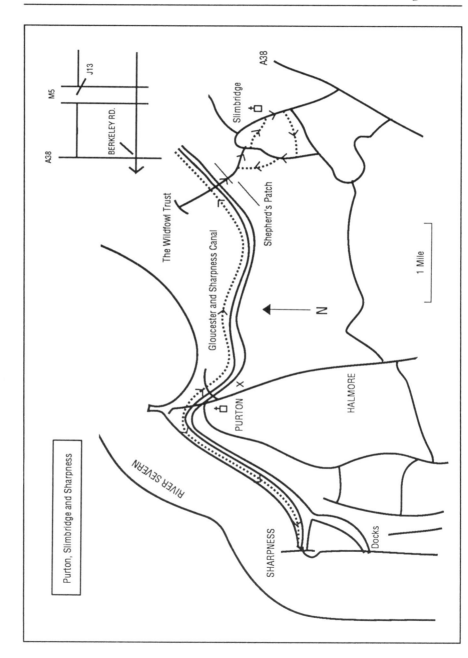

Bear right and then cross to the Church of St John the Evangelist. St John's dates from the twelfth, thirteenth and fourteenth centuries and deserves a prolonged browse. According to the Rector, the church is opened at 0900, daily. In case of disappointment, it is worth trying the Rectory – through a pair of white gates at the back of the churchyard – where the keys may be obtained. An excuse, if one is needed, for a stroll around the outside of the church: the tower and spire are particularly impressive. Returning, you will see the remains of a moat on the far side. This is where a manor house once stood.

Back at the entrance – the south porch – signs of wear and tear – several headless gargoyles and a sixteenth-century sundial. Inside, a booklet may be purchased for a pound. There are also 'bat notes' for reference. A notice on a column lists Rectors from the twelfth century to the present day. Further to your left, stands a lead font dated 1664. Columns ... arches ... two arcades run north and south of the nave. On the far side – there is a fine stained glass window in the north wall. Walking east, view the piano, organ, and Commandments One to Four. Into the chancel, see two piscinas, and a fourteenth century triple sedilia with three blue cushions. Returning along the south aisle, there are Commandments Five to Ten. Look up – and sixteen carved corbel heads – fourteenth century, white stone faces, look down.

Leave via the gates near the south porch. Almost opposite is a signposted footpath. Over the stile and proceed south-west, on through a gate – some new housing on the left – over a wooden footbridge – two more 'wooden constructions' that pass as stiles, to another of metal and wood. Here, follow the yellow arrow-head to your right. Walk west, close to a barbed-wire fence. Where the wire disappears into the undergrowth, you will see a concrete post sporting a large yellow spot. Pause, and take a bearing, south-south-west, give or take a degree. You should be able to see another splash of yellow in the distance, just to the left of a telegraph pole. Cross the field (currently ploughed and muddy) and climb the stile. Turn right, here, north-west, ignoring the path directly ahead to the road. Keep close to the hedge and make for a rusty old windmill, where again you change direction – west – see the yellow spot? It seems miles away. Cross to where a couple of railway sleepers straddle the ditch, and continue to a footbridge and Lightenbrook Lane.

Turn right and, further along, look carefully for a stile set in the hedge on your left. Up and over, a yellow arrow-head points north-west across fields to the road. Bear left, here, and it is only a matter of yards to Shepherd's Patch. More tea? Finally, retrace your steps back along the canal path – incidentally, part of the Severn Way Path – to Purton.

At Purton, if you have the time and energy, or another day to spare, there is the aforementioned optional extra. Instead of returning to the car park, continue along the canal path, past Purton Lower (no name on the bridge, but that is what it is called), the dredging barges and on to Sharpness. The area around Purton is noted for its many wooden barges – skeletons – relics of earlier times – lying half-buried and immobile in the river mud. RIP; they are an attractive sight, and even in death serve a purpose, helping to protect the banks from the scouring action of the Severn. At Sharpness, there is a marina, stacked with boats, beyond which the canal empties into the river. Here, it is preferable to retrace your steps back along the canal path to Purton. A circle is less than ideal – the docks do not exactly have eye appeal and many of the footpaths start with good intentions but soon peter out.

Note: Remember the cuppa at Shepherd's Patch? Try Buttons Camping Discount Centre. It is from a machine but cheap and very welcome. Loiter within tent. Currently, the Centre is closed on Wednesdays.

Boat trips are available at Shepherd's Patch. Daily during the summer and at weekends in the winter.

17. Berkeley and Stone

The walk starts in Berkeley, of castle fame, following the banks of the Little Avon River to Stone. It then stretches across fields to Hystfield, up and along Berkeley Deer Park (Whitcliff, on the map) and back through the attractive village of Ham. Appropriately, the walk is roughly bell-shaped – two of the three optional extras are churches. The third is slightly different – a Butterfly Farm. Watch the butterflies flutter by. The choice is yours, but I have assumed that you will first want to look at Berkeley's church, and then visit the Butterfly Farm. The Jenner Museum and Berkeley Castle are not included in the walk; the latter, in particular, deserves a day of its own. If you are here in the morning, you will have to leave the Butterfly Farm until the end of the walk, for it does not open until midday, and then only from April to October.

Route: Berkeley – Berkeley Castle – Stone – Whitcliff Deer Park – Ham – Berkeley

Distance: About 7 miles

Map: O.S. Landranger 162

Start: See *Parking*

Terrain: Generally level walking. In wet weather, some sticky patches and long, soaking grass across fields.

Nearest Towns: Bristol, Dursley, Gloucester, Stroud.

Access: Taking the A38, from Bristol to Gloucester, turn left just beyond Stone – the minor road north, through Ham to Berkeley.

Parking: Entering Berkeley along High Street, turn left into Canonbury Street then follow the road around to the right into Marybrook Street. A free car park is signposted on your right. There are Public Toilets opposite.

Public Transport: Ring Gloucester County Council on 0452 425543

Refreshments: Plenty of pubs. A fish and chip shop.

The Walk

Leaving the car park [see Parking], turn left along Marybrook Street and follow the road around into Canonbury Street. Cross and go down High Street, then left into Church Lane, walking past the Jenner Museum to the churchyard. History and humour: the tomb of Dicky Pearce, England's last court jester lies here. Continue past the 18th-century bell tower which contains a peal of ten bells (audibly bell-shaped), on to The Minster Church of St Mary the Virgin.

There is a plentiful supply of leaflets available to tell you all you need to know, but who can resist a brief summary? The church dates from the twelfth century and really is a step back in time. Thirteenth century wall paintings and much stunningly beautiful stained glass. A Norman font stands near the south wall. The tomb of Lord Thomas Berkeley (1361) and Lady Katherine Berkeley (1385) lies along the south aisle. Advancing a few centuries, the organ, built by Abbot and Smith of Leeds, dates from 1890. Its history, together with a list of past organists is on a board nearby. But this is just scratching the surface – buy a leaflet and browse. Preserving history is not cheap – at the time of writing, an appeal to restore the interior decoration, the south wall and the roof timbers has raised a considerable sum. More is needed – feel free.

Leave the church and just before the bell tower take the path right, approaching a small bridge. Go through a door in the wooden fence on your right, and then left over the bridge, along the car park to the Butterfly Farm.

Fifty pence and cheap at the price, but don't bother with a coat – butterflies like it hot. The Farm contains over forty species of butterfly, a breeding cage and even a few nuzzling zebra finches. It assails the eye, rather, watching hundreds of semitransparent, multicoloured wings fluttering all around one.

Retrace your steps to Church Lane and bear left to High Street. Left, again, walking past Jumpers Lane, down to a footpath, signposted Woodford. Cross the field, direction approximately south. Glancing to your left you will see Berkeley Castle – and very impressive it is, too.

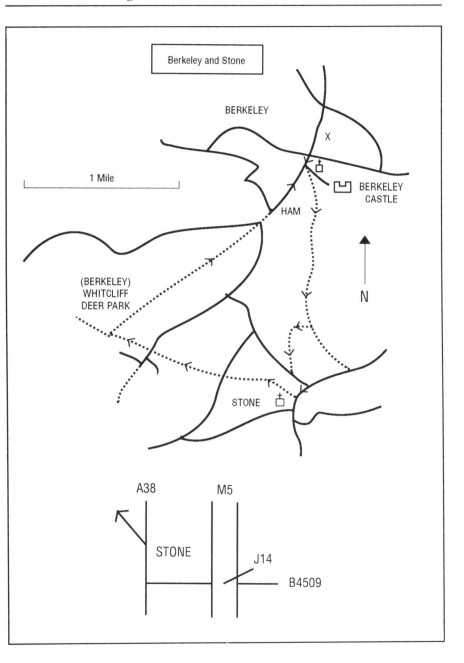

Cannons at Berkeley Castle

The path brings you to a bridge – do not cross – continue straight on, over a stile, walking alongside the Little Avon River. Like walkers, stiles come in all shapes and sizes. The next one is nothing more than three pieces of wood between two posts. There are a few such along this walk, so you will need to be fairly agile. In this instance, however, it is easier to go through the gate on your left. Continue straight ahead, admiring, in passing, the silvery-leaved willows on the bank, opposite. Approaching Brownsmill Farm, go straight across – over the fence, the lane and a second fence, still keeping to the left of the river. A 'proper' stile, under large willows, is crossed as you walk south-south-west; you can see the spire of Stone's church in the distance.

This fairly long stretch ends at a bridge, a metal gate and a yellow arrow-head on a post. Cross the river, not forgetting to close the gate, for there are cattle and sheep grazing, and turn immediately left to a stile. Up and over, bearing right, due west, along the edge of a field, keeping the hedge to your right. A couple of right angles to a fence-cum-stile – harder to climb, this one. Take the direction indicated by the arrow-head, making for a spot just to the right of a clump of trees. Through the gate – not literally – it is kept padlocked open, following the barbed wire fence around to the road. Left, here, and take care, the road is narrow and the occasional car whizzes by. Continue past the school to the A38.

Turn right – a few yards further stands All Saints' Church, Stone. Enter via the south porch. If locked, the key may be obtained from Church House. The church dates from the thirteenth century; tower and spire were added around 1400. Something of an anticlimax after Berkeley, perhaps, but there are several interesting features described in a leaflet which may be purchased for a few pence.

Leave the church, bearing right to the west gate and the road. Right, here, for a few yards only, and where the road winds left, take the narrow road, right, due north. Dare I say: exercise special care along this section to Hystfield. Despite compass and map, I took a wrong turning. A farmer scathingly remarked to my eternal shame: 'Lost, are you?'

Proceed to the entrance of Westend House, through the gate, bearing left off the drive, under an arch of tasty blackberries, and over the stile. Follow the direction of the arrow-head, north-north-west, across the field to an unusual combination of sleeper and fence – walk up the sleeper and climb over the fence, and then bear slightly left, on to a footbridge. Cross this, walking west, and keep just to the right of a facing hedge, to the road.

Over the stile, opposite, and turn right, passing close to a house and 'through' the remains of a stile. Take a bearing north-west – you should see a splash of yellow and a footbridge in the hedge. Once over, go immediately right, keeping the hedge to your right, on through a patch of rough ground (nettles, brambles), another footbridge and straight across a field to, in quick succession – stile, two sleepers and stile. Next, make for the telegraph pole in the middle of the field, direction west. From here, you should be able to see the beginnings of a footbridge in the far hedge. Don't despair, it can be hidden by the summer's growth – just continue to the hedge and cast about a few yards. You are now at the last field before the road. Make for a point just to the right of a pair of white houses – again west, passing a yellow arrow-head stamped on a telegraph pole. At last – one more stile and the road.

Bear right, then left, taking the signposted footpath up a field – the only moderately steep section of the walk. At the top, climb the stile, but don't follow the track around to your right, continue up, north-west, passing an arrow-head on a post, around and along by a red brick wall. More stiles, then up the steps and over the wall into Berkeley Deer Park.

As the name implies, you may be lucky enough to glimpse the deer that roam the area. Proceed north-east along the wide track – you can see the River Severn between trees to your left; and further on, a building looking more like a rook in a giant's chess set. Keep to the right of a long line of mostly horse chestnut (conkers galore in the autumn), still walking north-east. Nearing the end of the trees, ignore the track that veers off to the right. Continue straight on – in the distance you can see Berkeley's church and castle. The track descends, joining another that ends at a lodge. Take the path that leads down to the wall – more steps – and along to the road.

Continue through Ham, past The Salutation and Hamlet Cottage, entering Berkeley by way of High Street, back to the start of the walk.

18. Marshfield and Cold Ashton

The walk starts in Marshfield, touches Dyrham Park, turns south along part of the Cotswold Way through Pennsylvania to Cold Ashton and then returns via Beek's Lane. Two churches, two villages, centuries-old buildings and much Cotswold stone. However, it is not the easiest of walks, especially during wet weather [see Terrain].

Route: Marshfield – Dyrham – Pennsylvania – Cold Ashton – Marshfield

Distance: About 8 miles

Map: O.S. Landranger 172

Start: See *Parking*

Terrain: Varied and fairly demanding in places. There are several steep sections; one, in particular, along Beek's Lane, towards the end of the walk. No shortage of mud, especially through the wood that lies across the Cotswold Way. Boots are strongly recommended. You may wish to take the more direct route – a footpath through the valley between Marshfield and Cold Ashton – it is marked on the Landranger map, but is exceptionally marshy and jungle-like in places. I safaried along in wet October. Perhaps the going is easier during a dry spell; of about ten years.

Nearest Towns: Yate, Bristol, Bath, Chippenham.

Access: A420 Bristol to Chippenham road. Marshfield is at map ref: 780738.

Parking: Off the A420, in the lay-by just to the east of Marshfield.

Public Toilets: In High Street

Public Transport: A few buses. Ring Gloucester County Council, 0452 425543.

Refreshments: Plenty of pubs in Marshfield, but best is the 'takeaway' in the lay-by. Excellent: they do two and four star breakfasts at any time of day. A 'semi-takeaway', for one may sit and dine in a café-cum-caravan. Orders will even be brought to your car. At the time of writing, a mug of tea is 25 pence, a third of what a pub (anon.) tried to charge me. Monday to Friday only, regrettably.

What's in a name? Marshy Marshfield, a large village lying in the Hundred of Edderstone. Although situated on high ground, the surrounding land can be what one may call soggy. Originally bisected by the busy A420, Marshfield has been bypassed, fortunately, leaving a wide street and many interesting buildings. Cold Ashton, too, is aptly described: in the winter months, it can be very cold indeed.

The Walk

Having parked and possibly enjoyed a mug of tea [see Parking and Refreshments], walk along Chippenham Road towards the village. Keeping left is the order of the day – around, past the Lord Nelson Inn, into Hay Street, coming finally to the Church of St Mary the Virgin, Marshfield.

Consecrated in 1242 by Walter de Cantaloupe, the Bishop of Worcester, the church underwent considerable alteration in the succeeding years. As you enter, the fifteenth-century font stands to your left. On your right, on the south wall, is a small brass to a distant relation of Guy Fawkes. Further along this wall is a fine stained glass window – a memorial to the late Canon Trotman. Approaching the altar, hangs a brass chandelier. Read the inscription: 'Mark Harvard and Edward Tiley, churchwardens 1725 – 1726.' It is lit during church festivals.

Leaving the church, retrace your steps as far as the Market Place and then keep left, into and along High Street. Hardly history, but you may see a plaque on the wall of a house: 'Winner of the Avon best kept large village 1988'. Continue past the Post Office, virtually to the end of the street, turning right into George Lane. The Almshouses stand on the corner – seventeenth-century Cotswold stone, topped by a small clock tower and spire. George Lane brings you to the A420 – cross with care to the road opposite and on to castellated Castle Farm. Again, go straight on – the narrow road ducks and weaves – past Springs Farm to high ground; a long stretch to the A46.

Take the road signposted Dyrham. On your right is Dyrham Park where you may glimpse grazing deer. The road descends – a couple of blind corners – and by the village sign, turn left, joining the Cotswold Way.

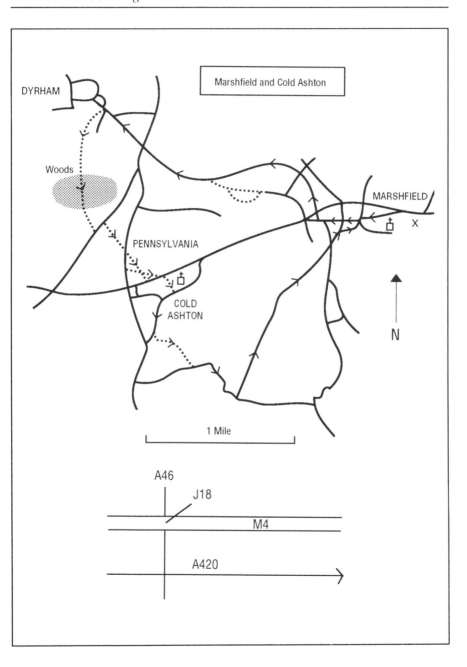

The Way is well signposted, so I will just touch the high spots. Approaching the wood, walking approximately south, you come to a yellow arrow-head on a post. Continue over the footbridge and up steps, along a tract of waste ground to a stile and the wood 'proper'. The ascent lasts no more than ten minutes but can be difficult, particularly in wet weather. The last part – little more than a gully – may be avoided by taking to the ground on your right. Beyond the wood, you will see a yellow right-angled arrow – walk to the right of the old farm building, keeping the hedge to your left, direction south-east, coming to a short but sometimes busy section of road. Follow the Way signs and take care, on through Pennsylvania, across fields that are often ploughed and sticky, to the Holy Trinity Church, Cold Ashton.

Church of the Holy Trinity, Cold Ashton

The church, except the tower, which probably dates from the fourteenth century, was rebuilt between 1508-1539 by the Rector, Thomas Key. He financed this rebuilding himself, though how he obtained the money is unknown. Inside is much beautiful stained glass. In a glass case is a volume of the original authorised version of the Bible.

Still following the Cotswold Way, continue through the churchyard, turning right at the road. You will see a white arrow-head stamped high on a telegraph pole. Leave the Way, here, taking the road left, direction south. Look for a buckled metal gate and yellow arrow-head on a post to your left. Go through and across the field, walking south-east, to a wooden gate and lane, initially quite muddy, which ends at Frys Farm and the road.

Bear left and negotiate the narrow road with care: winding and descending a 1 in 5 gradient, down to the Monkswood Springwater Reservoir. Further on, you will see a sign: 'Beek's Mill – bridleway only – please shut gate'. Thinking horsy thoughts, turn left along this lane. The rough surface soon acquires a coat of tarmac and ascends, steeply. This section will really test your stamina.

The gradient eases, passing several old railway wagons and an eighteenth-century stone pillar. Walking along here in the autumn, I'm sure you will be unable to resist the edible, fruity freebies – blackberries, that fill both hedges. Beyond Knowle Hill Farm, you can see the tower of Marshfield's church in the distance. Turn left at the junction – Marshfield Cricket Club is opposite – and right along Sheepfair Lane, up to High Street, back to the start of the walk. Another mug of tea? Why not; you deserve it.

19. Bourton-on-the-Water and The Slaughters

For the most part, one leaves Bourton-on-the-Water with pleasant memories: of the River Windrush that meanders through the town, with its chubby ducks and low stone bridges; of the Model Village, the Model Railway, Birdland and so on. But other memories intrude: the massive car parks, the daily influx of tourists, the way many of the houses have been spoilt by commercialism. Despite this, Bourton still has much to offer. It is best visited mid-week, between late autumn and early spring.

The walk starts in Bourton, takes the Oxfordshire Way (in Gloucestershire) to Wyck Rissington, passes through Lower and Upper Slaughter and returns. There are three rivers to cross and four churches to visit, enough for anyone, I hope.

Route: Bourton-on-the-Water – Wyck Rissington – Lower Slaughter – Upper Slaughter – Bourton-on-the-Water

Distance: About 7 miles

Map: O.S. Landranger 163

Start: See *Parking*

Terrain: Mostly level with some muddy patches. Boots are recommended.

Nearest Towns: Cirencester, Cheltenham, Stow-on-the-Wold

Access: Bourton-on-the-Water is well signposted and lies just off the A429 between Cirencester and Stow-on-the-Wold at map ref: 168208.

Parking: This is a problem, particularly during the busy summer months. It is possible to find a side street, but more convenient to use a Pay and Display. Having turned off the A429, along Station Road, you cannot miss Bourton Vale Car Park – on your right, behind the garage. At the time of writing, a fairly modest £2 buys you up to 6 hours. There are also public toilets.

Public Transport: A few buses, mostly privately operated. Ring Gloucester County Council on 0452 425543.

Refreshments: A full range is available in Bourton.

The Walk

Having denounced the car parks, I am starting the walk from one of them [see Parking]. Make for Station Road, cross to the pavement and bear left, a matter of yards to where a green signpost, opposite, points to Wyck Rissington. Go right here, joining the Oxfordshire Way along a road called 'Roman Way' – confusing – and then right again into Moor Lane. A few yards further, stone steps lead up and around to a stile. This section to Wyck Rissington is well-signposted – a succession of stiles and gates across fields, and old railway sleepers and footbridges over the rivers Eye and Dikler. A walk of about thirty minutes to the road, where stands a letter-box, tastefully painted a flaking red.

Bridge over the River Windrush, Bourton

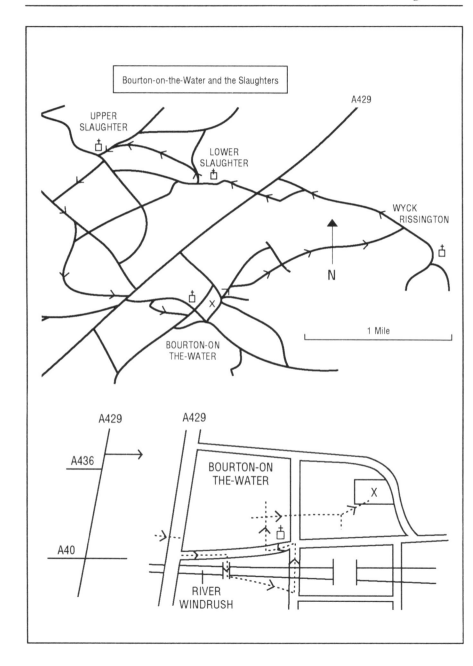

Bourton-on-the-Water and the Slaughters

Turn right along the road to the Church of St Laurence, Wyck Rissington. No shortage of leaflets; to summarise: the church is of Saxon origins, was rebuilt in Norman times and has undergone various alterations since. The walls of the tower are 9 feet thick at the base. The beautiful stained glass contains fourteenth century fragments. On a musical note, planetary Gustav Holst was organist here for a while in his youth. In 1950, Canon Harry Cheales planted a maze in the Rectory gardens. He was given exact instructions regarding its design in a dream. When the Canon retired in 1980, the rectory was sold and the maze destroyed. You can see a scaled down plan of this maze – a mosaic – in the north wall of the nave.

Leaving the church, retrace your steps back along the road, past the letter-box, saying good-bye to the Oxfordshire Way. Walk north-west, and negotiate a series of bends with care, over a bridge – the railway, below, has long gone, but at least the sleepers have been put to good use. Beyond the bridge, turn left along the signposted bridleway – a wide, grassy tract, through a gate and over the Dikler. There are ponies and horses to right and left as you walk around to your right, and then a choice of gate or stile, coming finally to the A429.

Cross with care, taking the road to Lower Slaughter. You can see the slender church spire above the trees as you approach the village. Attractive, certainly, with houses dating from the sixteenth century, but tourism and property development have taken their toll. Evidence of the motor car – yellow lines along the roads – hardly add eye appeal. Pass Lower Slaughter Manor and bear right through the churchyard to St Mary's Church.

The thirteenth century church was rebuilt in the 1860s at the expense of the Whitmore family, who occupied the manor from the early seventeenth century to the 1960s. The arches between the aisles still retain their thirteenth century origins.

Leave the churchyard by the other gate, direction west. Turn right along the road, on to where it curves sharply to the right. Here, take the footpath straight ahead – north-west – another well-signposted section, across fields, coming finally to a swing gate and a narrow stone bridge over the river to the road. Bear left, to the square and up through the churchyard surrounded by attractive cottages with roofs of Cotswold stone – to the Church of St Peter, Upper Slaughter.

The church dates from Norman times and was restored in the nineteenth century. Inside, see the two stained glass windows on your right, the south wall: running from left to right – the four evangelists – Saints Matthew, Mark, Luke and John. In the chapel to the north of the chancel stands the black, marble-topped tomb of the Reverend Francis Edward Witts, rector of the parish for 46 years.

Back at the road, turn right and then left at the T-junction, on past Lavender Cottage, taking the road right, direction south-west, signposted Guiting Power and Winchcombe. This is a long, gentle ascent – well, it seems gentle, but the further one goes, the steeper it gets. Looking back, it appears almost precipitous. I walked along here one day in the autumn, stopping to munch blackberries. Unhappily, the next week they had all gone, victim of the hedge trimmer.

Bear left at the T-junction. The occasional car passes, and it is preferable to ignore the Highway Code, keeping to the left, mostly on a grass verge. A couple of minutes, only, to where you cross to the signposted bridleway, direction south. An unsurfaced lane beside a field – a gentle descent, this time. On through several metal gates and around an old wooden one, the lane narrows to a sort of 'path T-junction'. Choose the left-hand path, over or through the gate (it can be very muddy) and along, direction south, veering south-east. More mud, brambles and nettles add to the joys of the walking experience. The path dips, briefly, to a small gate beside a blue arrow-head on a post. Continue, walking along the edge of a field, towards the A429 and Bourton, with the River Windrush to your right and the banks of that old railway to your left.

A last stile brings you to the road. Cross with care to the right-hand pavement of the road opposite – Lansdowne, a walk of five minutes to a signposted footpath on your right. Continue over the small bridge, walking alongside the river. The path ends in Sherborne Street. Left, here, over that river again, down to the War Memorial, where you turn left, back along Lansdowne, crossing to the other pavement. By the last of the parked cars, take the footpath right to the Church of St Lawrence. The church entrance is around to your right, the south porch.

There has been much rebuilding on early eighth century foundations over the years. The chancel was rebuilt in 1328 by Walter de Burhton; the tower is eighteenth century; the rest mostly nineteenth century. The tower has a peal of 8 bells, and a carillon which plays seven hymns, one for each day of the week. Be here on the hour and you will hear it.

Leaving the church, take the path immediately right, direction north, and at the 'path crossroads' bear right, direction east, straight across Moore Road and left by some allotments, back to the car park.

20. Guiting Power and Naunton

This roughly triangular walk in the north of Gloucestershire passes through Guiting Power and Naunton, villages lying in the Hundreds of Holford and Greston, respectively. A stroll of about two hours, plus church browsing time. Perish the thought, but should you get lost and need to use the word 'Guiting', it is pronounced as in the Guy of Fawkes; so I was advised by a gentleman in Naunton Post Office. Thank you, sir; henceforth, I walk corrected.

Route: Guiting Power – Naunton – Guiting Power

Distance: About 5 miles

Map: O.S. Landranger 163

Start: See *Parking*

Terrain: Mostly level with occasional muddy patches

Nearest Towns: Cirencester, Cheltenham, Stow-on-the-Wold

Access: Travelling along the A429 between Cirencester and Stow-on-the-Wold, take the minor road left, signposted Naunton, opposite Bourton-on-the-Water, at map ref: 161211. Then left, again, at the B4068 and the third road right – the first two lead to Naunton. Another right, and a left opposite Guiting Stud brings you to Guiting Power.

Parking: Entering Guiting Power, bear left a few yards past the Farmer's Arms, by Watsons Bakers and Grocers. Keep straight on, down to the church, map ref: 096246.

Public Transport: A few buses, privately operated, to Bourton and Cheltenham. Ring Gloucester County Council on 0452 425543.

Refreshments: The Farmer's Arms in Guiting Power. Nuts and so forth may be purchased from Watsons or the Post Office.

The River Windrush, Naunton

The Walk

I hope that you have been successful in negotiating the tangled spaghetti of roads in the area [see Access and Parking]. Legs at the ready, you are standing near the battlemented tower of St Michael's Church, Guiting Power. A visit before the walk seems a good idea – through the churchyard, past a variegated holly and around to the porch. A leaflet is available for a few pence, but just in case:

Briefly, the church is Norman in origin and has undergone much alteration in the succeeding years. To accommodate an increasing population, north and south transepts were added in the nineteenth century. Face the altar and admire the beautiful stained glass and, by contrast, a child's stone coffin beside the pulpit. The coffin is believed to be Saxon.

Retrace your steps to the road and bear immediately left, over a stile, direction south. As the sign reveals, this is part of the Wardens' Way. The path dips, passing Guiting Power Nature Reserve, and then ascends, up steps, opening onto a field, currently ploughed and extremely muddy in wet weather.

Where the path ends, pause to scrape the boots and then take the road opposite, signposted Naunton and Stow-on-the-Wold. A few minutes' walk to another Wardens' Way sign that directs left, across more fields, passing a post with a yellow arrow-head and green 'W' at its centre. Looking down to your left, you can see the River Windrush winding along the Windrush valley. You reach a hurdle of sorts that has to be climbed, and turn left, down the road into Naunton. Keep to the road where it curves around to the left, leaving the Wardens' Way, and then left, again, up to the Church of St Andrew, Naunton.

Inside, there are notes for reference, but not to be taken away. Incidentally, if you are really interested, a booklet may be purchased for £2 from the Post Office. Guiting Power and Naunton are fortunate in still having a Post Office. The church is believed to date from the twelfth century, but was mostly rebuilt in the fifteenth and sixteenth centuries and underwent restoration in 1899. It boasts an impressive carved stone pulpit dating from about 1400. On the north wall are two brasses to Ann Major and Leticia Holt. You can read the details for yourselves. Leaving

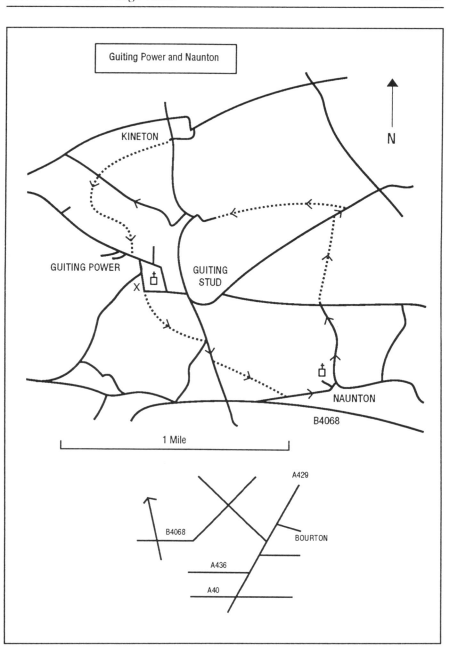

the church, walk around to the right – the fifteenth century tower is not only battlemented, but pinnacled and 'gargoyled' as well. Additionally, there are two sundials, dated 1748, painted on the south and west walls. The last time I visited, the sun obligingly shone at twelve on a wet November's day, casting an accurate shadow on the south wall.

Return to the road and bear left, over the river, and a few yards further, left again, by Sheepwell Cottage, direction north. Ascending to the T-junction, continue straight ahead, along an unsurfaced lane – a long stretch of high ground. Don't get caught here without a waterproof when the heavens open. At the road, bear right for about a hundred yards, and then left along another lane, direction west. The lane descends, finally winding down into Barton.

Turn right, over the bridge, and left by a sign 'Unsuitable for heavy goods vehicles'. Not being HGV one need not worry too much. Later, one can see the reason for the sign – the lane is a bit 'crumbly' and acquires a central grass strip. Should you want to shorten the walk, you will pass a footpath on your left that leads to Guiting Power. However, being made of sterner stuff, you will no doubt continue, passing a friendly stable: one of the horses always came up to me to say hello. What is horse for carrot, I wonder?

At Castlett Farm, take the signposted footpath, left, through the farm entrance (there is no gate). Keep left at the fork, and where the gravel path bears right, into the yard, go straight on – south – along a grassy path, a bridleway. Two red/brown arrow-heads on the fence direct south-west, through a gate, entering a short wooded section. The path descends, becoming soggy underfoot, and heads over the small bridge and around to the left.

Leaving the trees, the path eventually joins a road, passing Castlett Lodge and Pilgrim Cottage (making good progress, here), and then left, down to just beyond the War Memorial – right at Watsons, back to the start of the walk.

21. Stanton and Stanway

This is a fairly short yet quite demanding walk. An opportunity to test the boots – the terrain is rough in places, with plenty of mud – cooling to the blood, by all accounts. By way of compensation, if any is needed, it is packed with interest. Clockwise, for a change, through Stanton and Stanway, twin jewels in the Cotswold crown. Also a walk slightly on the wild side – across Shenberrow Camp and down through Lidcombe Wood, part of the Stanway Estate. Intriguingly, you may also hear a train whistle.

Route: Stanton – Lidcombe Wood – Stanway – Stanton

Distance: About 5 miles

Map: O.S. Landranger 150

Start: See *Parking*

Terrain: One long ascent out of Stanton. Plenty of mud and rough underfoot in places. Boots are strongly recommended.

Nearest Towns: Broadway, Cheltenham, Evesham, Tewkesbury

Access: At junction 9 of the M5, take the A438 and B4077 to where it is crossed by the B4632 (the old A46 beyond Cheltenham). First left, here, at the roundabout – the B4632 to Broadway. Stanton is signposted a mile or so on your right.

Parking: Entering Stanton, continue through the village, around to your left – there is a sign on the wall. The car park lies in front of Stanton Village Club. It is small, so get there early.

Public Transport: A few buses, privately operated. Castleways, I think; best to ring Gloucester County Council on 0452 425543.

Refreshments: The Mount Inn, passed during the walk.

The Walk

Leave the car park [see Parking], and turn right along the road, following it around to the left, as far as the village cross – medieval, with a seventeenth century sundial and globe. Left, here, through the churchyard to the Church of St Michael, Stanton.

Pleasure, delectation, delight – even from the outside, the church catches the eye. Pure Cotswolds: of twelfth century origins, with some later alterations and additions. The tower is topped by a finely proportioned spire; the south porch is lined with battlements and pinnacles. A browse within should not be missed. Approaching the altar, you will see traces of a fourteenth century wall painting on the north wall of the north transept, and can also look along a passage squint. There are two pulpits: the smaller one on your left is fourteenth century; the other, with its two brass candle holders (whose lampshades hide light bulbs), dates from the seventeenth century. There is another 'non-passage' squint in the south transept. The small windows in the east walls of both transepts are by Sir Ninian Comper. The south bears his familiar 'trademark', a wild strawberry, dotted around the window.

Return to the street and bear left, direction east, walking briefly along the Cotswold Way. It is difficult not to rhapsodise. Who cannot fail to appreciate the perfection of the street itself? Every house different, yet blending to form a whole; a rich tapestry in yellow stone.

Leave the Way where the road forks, bearing left, the start of the only ascent of the walk – a fairly long one, too. Up the narrow road, and the path and steps by Mount Inn. Beyond, take the signposted footpath, again east. This is often muddy and always rough underfoot – a taste of things to come. Take care opening the first gate, it drops alarmingly on one hinge. Ignore the yellow arrow-head that points right, keeping straight on. Looking back, you can see a viaduct in the distance. Continue through two more gates – the path widens to an unsurfaced lane, veers south-east and eases to a more gentle ascent. A few yards beyond the third gate you rejoin the Cotswold Way, turning right, direction initially south-west. This is high, sheep-grazing country – in winter, the wind can cut like a knife.

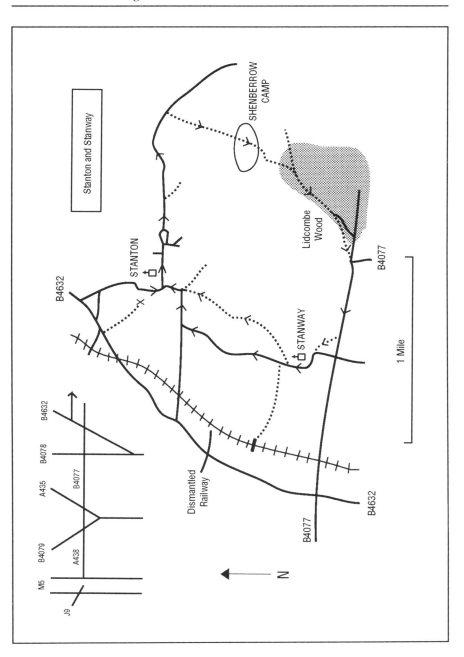

Stanton and Stanway

SHENBERROW CAMP

STANTON

Lidcombe Wood

STANWAY

B4632

B4077

1 Mile

Dismantled Railway

B4632

B4077

N

M5 · J9 · B4079 · A438 · A435 · B4078 · B4077 · B4632

Eventually, you cross Shenberrow Camp – an Iron Age hill fort of about three acres in area. Excavations in 1935 unearthed, among other things, pottery, bone needles, a bronze bracelet and a tanged iron knife.

At the gate beside the farm, a yellow arrow-head with a white spot in the middle directs – beyond, a way post points down, but leave the Way here, continuing straight ahead – south – following a path through trees. Where the path veers west, keep south, to a gate and stile. Two arrow-heads, this time. Up and over (masses of mud), taking the right-hand path – south – across a patch of rough ground, through an opening in the hedge where a gate once stood, entering Lidcombe Wood. Bear right at the fork.

A long descent – very rough and muddy (boots really are a must, here). Walk quietly, for there is plenty of wildlife to see and hear; a pump, too, thumping away in the distance. Reaching the edge of the wood, the track bears sharply left, and then right, towards a green-topped post. Take the gate a few yards before this post, walking west, now, past Papermill Farm to the road.

Turn right along the pavement, on to where the road is crossed by the omnipresent Cotswold Way. Right, here, over the stile, following the Way signs, passing the imposing south gate of Stanway House to the Church of St Peter, Stanway.

You may want to take advantage of the enormous scraper by the porch. The church was rebuilt in the twelfth century and restored in 1896. Consequently, it looks rather 'new' inside. There is one notable exception: approaching the chancel, you can see traces of a seventeenth century wall painting on the north-west wall of the chancel arch, above and behind the pulpit.

Leaving the church, turn right along the road. Further along, on your left, you will see what looks like a barn with a thatched roof, standing on staddle stones. These were used to keep mice and rats at bay. It is, in fact, a cricket pavilion.

At this point, I offer a choice – wet or dry. One may bear right across fields, taking the Cotswold Way back to Stanton – very 'soggy' walking in the winter. The second, and to me, preferable option, is just to continue along the road. The occasional car and horse pass, but it is a pleasant enough twenty-minute walk which brings you to a T-junction. Turn right – the Cotswold Way joins the road further on – then around left, through the village, back to the start of the walk.

Cotswold housing, Stanton

A note for pedestrian railway buffs: it is possible to take a footpath west from the car park in Stanton to the old Gloucestershire and Warwickshire Railway. You can then walk south along the track bed as far as the viaduct, seen as you ascend out of Stanton. There is a rather awkward descent just before the viaduct and a bridleway back to the road.

Did you hear a train whistle, and wonder? Or did you know all along? As yet another optional extra, why not visit the Gloucestershire Warwickshire Railway near Toddington? Privately operated, mostly steam trains run between Toddington, Winchcombe and Gretton from March to October. There are also Santa Specials in December. An extension towards Cheltenham is planned. Become a member and get involved. According to the leaflet, all tasks from Engine Driver to Station Cleaner are carried out by volunteers. Ring 0242 621405 for more information.

22. Winchcombe

This walk is quite demanding in places, but full of interest – you will visit a church, pass close to a castle and enjoy the panoramic Cotswolds – I hope.

Route: Winchcombe – Winchcombe Church – Studeley Lodge – Winchcombe

Distance: About 7 miles

Map: O.S. Landranger 163

Start: See *Parking*

Terrain: From rough to sticky to firm underfoot. The first part is a mix of ascents and mud; the second, mostly level and mud. Ultra muddy in wet weather – don't forget the boots and waterproofs. You will probably walk this during a hot, dry spell, when clay turns to cracked concrete, and wonder what all the fuss is about.

Nearest towns: Cheltenham, Evesham, Tewkesbury

Access: I prefer junction 9 of the M5, and then A438, B4077 and B4078. You can, of course, take a more direct route: the A46, which after passing through a nightmare of one-way streets in Cheltenham, becomes the B4632 and enters Winchcombe from the south. Winchcombe is at approximate map ref: 025285.

Parking: Entering Winchcombe from the north, along the B4078, you will come to a crossroad and should see a Long Stay car park sign. Follow, going straight across into Back Lane. The park, which is free, is on your left, but arrive early. Environmentally sound can, bottle and paper banks are there to be used. Public Toilets are near the entrance to Vineyard Street.

Public Transport: A limited bus service. Ring Gloucester County Council on 0452 425543

Refreshments: Plenty of pubs and restaurants

Winchcombe lies in the Hundred of Greston and has origins stretching back to the earliest of times. In the eighth century, Winchcombe was a Saxon town of some standing: a nunnery was established by King Offa in 787; Winchcombe Abbey was founded by King Kenulf and dedicated in 811 by the Archbishop of Canterbury. The abbey flourished, and the town with it. Visiting pilgrims and scholars would stay, but the town's prosperity was always 'in the shadow' of the abbey. In the long term, this proved to be something of a handicap, for the town never developed its own industry or took full advantage of the wool trade. So, although a useful source of income, relations between town and abbey were often less than ideal. Finally, in 1539, the abbey was confiscated by Henry VIII's commissioners. Thereafter, Winchcombe went into a long decline. Tobacco was grown in the early seventeenth century, but eventually suppressed by a Government with colonies in Virginia to maintain, and Winchcombe did not really recover until Victorian times.

Gargoyle, Church of St Peter, Winchcombe

The Walk

Leave the car park, walking away from the school, direction east, and turn right along Cowl Lane, past Stone Cottage and Winchcombe Parish Hall to High Street. Bear right, beyond Queen's Square, along to the Parish Church of St Peter, Winchcombe.

St Peter's dates from around 1465 and should not be missed. A brief conducted tour follows: first, through the south porch and around to your left, where a leaflet may be purchased for a mere ten pence and a more detailed booklet for a pound from the 'Church Shop'. There are birthday cards, too, and cheap at the price. The font's stone pedestal dates from 1634; the bowl is a replacement, but the blue cover an original. The first of two stone coffins, reputedly that of King Kenulf, stands at the west end of the south aisle. A second stone coffin, reputedly that of Kenulf's son, Kenelm, murdered when a child, stands at the end of the north aisle. Along the north wall, you will see an oak door from Winchcombe Abbey; an almsbox with three locks – it could only be opened in the presence of the Vicar and two churchwardens; and an altar cloth in a glass case (behind curtains) which dates from the fourteenth century. Continuing past the eighteenth century organ, one comes to the chancel. On the north side, there is a kneeling effigy of Sir Thomas Williams of Corndean, who died in 1636. The beautiful stained glass of the east window depicts Jesus stilling the storm and St Peter's attempt to walk on water. On the south side of the chancel are a piscina and a triple sedilia with seats for the priests. Walking back along the nave you will see a chandelier, dated 1753, and read the inscription: *'The Gift of Jn. Merryman to Winchcomb Church, 1753'.*

Additionally, the church deserves a walk around the outside. There are battlements, pinnacles, forty gargoyles, some of which are said to caricature locals of the day, and a tower topped by a gilded weathercock, brought from St Mary Redcliffe Church, Bristol.

Leaving the church, bear left and then right into Vineyard Street which, incidentally, is part of the Cotswold Way and also the road to Sudeley Castle. The castle is not included in the walk, but can be visited outside the winter months, for a fee. Leave the Way as you approach the lodge, continuing along the road that passes just to the right of the lodge – the

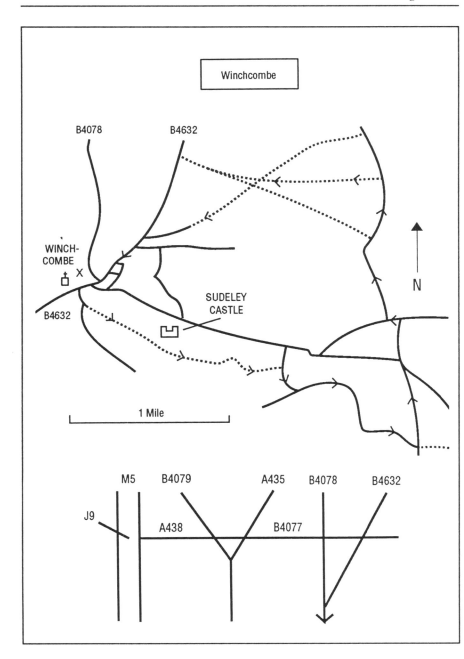

Wardens' Way, this time. On through a gate with a *'Please Latch'* sign and along the road. Keep to the grass verge in the summer, as this is the main route for cars to the castle, and along an avenue of chestnuts – read all about them on the bridge. You come to two gates – take the right-hand one, still the Wardens' Way – the path leads across a field and offers free castellated views. Keep the fence close to your left to the point where it 'right-angles' away, and then strike across the field, direction south-south-east, making for the corner diagonally opposite. You will not see the stile until you are almost upon it. Beware: the field is very sticky in wet weather and is home to some very active moles.

Climb the stile and go immediately left along to another. The ground can be very muddy here – top soil washed down by heavy rain. Two discs, two choices: right or straight on – take the latter, the Wardens' Way. Up and over, along the edge of a field with the wire fence to your left, walking east. Don't go through the gate at the end but bear right, taking care to avoid the deep ditch. Go left, across a couple of railway sleepers, over another stile and then a fairly gentle ascent to the road.

Right, here, and along to Sudeley Lodge. You will see a stone tablet set in the wall to your right: *'In Aug. 1788 George III visited this house ... on his way from Sudeley Castle to Brockhampton Park'.* Pass through the grounds and around, ascending, still following the Wardens' Way – there are stunning views across the valley. The lane levels and traces a long, lazy curve around to Park's Farm. Approaching, you pass a barn of sweet-smelling hay and the lane loses its tarmac surface. Beyond, bear left, another ascent, rough underfoot, a longish stretch to trees. Keep right through the open gate – one final ascent with woodland on your left – and the lane levels to the road.

The remainder of the walk is mostly level, you will be glad to hear. Turn left along the road, on to where it joins another, signposted 'Winch-combe and Cheltenham'. The occasional car passes, but a grass verge is conveniently 'to foot'. Then right – the road signposted 'Ford and Cutsdean', direction north. Bear left at the T-junction and about fifty yards further, right along the road signposted 'Little Farmcote'. At the time of writing, the sign lies on the ground. As an additional reference, there is also a triangular 'gates' sign. This is high, level ground – exposed, too; don't forget the waterproofs, just in case. Further along, ignore the signposted footpath to your left, continuing straight ahead.

The road descends to a large stone and the words: *'Little Farmcote to your right, public road to your left'*; so keep left, through a gate, ignoring another signposted footpath to right and left, on down to yet another signposted footpath – white walkers etched in wood. Bear left, direction west, taking to the grass again.

Over a stile and across the field, following the faint outline of the path, being sure to keep just to the left of a 'hedge' of trees that also points west. Pass between trees to another stile. Here, the path follows a line close to the fence on your right, but it is easier to avoid the muddier stretches, keeping to the higher ground, still walking west. Towards the end of the field there is an open gate on your right. You cannot see it, yet, but on the far side of one of the gate-posts is a disc, arrow-head and the encouraging words: 'Landowners welcome caring walkers'. A choice – one can go through this gate and immediately left, or avoid the mud and continue a few yards further, easily 'stepping' over the fence. Still walking west, you come to a pair of gates – through, bearing right, slightly – one last gate and down the field, which opens onto another, passing to the left of an old barn. In the distance, you should be able to make out a stile and white disc – closer inspection reveals a yellow arrow-head with a white spot in its centre; the Cotswold Way (again). Over the stile and along the path to a final stile and Puck Pit Lane; initially quite rough and muddy, but the worst may be avoided by keeping to the right.

At the road, the B4632, keep a wary eye open for traffic, cross to the pavement opposite and turn left into Winchcombe. There is newer housing, on the outskirts of the town. Cross over the River Isbourne, head on past Kenulf Road to the start of older housing. Broadway Road becomes Hailes Street and you are approaching what used to be the George Hotel, originally built as an inn for pilgrims. Gone, now, converted to flats, but still with a sign depicting St George slaying the dragon. Past the Tourist Office, the sixteenth-century, timber-framed Wesley House Restaurant, to just beyond Winchcombe Methodist Church, where you see the sign 'High Street' on the wall of a bank. Opposite is Cowl Lane. Right, along here, back to the start of the walk.

23. Withington and Chedworth Villa

This is a walk that is best saved for the quieter months – late autumn to early spring. In outline, a piece from a jigsaw puzzle, which starts in Withington and winds clockwise, around to Chedworth Villa, through Withington Woods and back again. There are the remains of one Roman Villa to see, if you wish, and, of course, St Michael's at Withington, kept to the very end.

Route: Withington – Chedworth Roman Villa – Chedworth Woods and Nature Reserve – Withington Woods – Withington

Distance: About 5 miles

Map: O.S. Landranger 163

Start: See *Parking*

Terrain: Reasonable, apart from the section through Withington Woods which is rough underfoot in places and often muddy. Boots are recommended.

Nearest Towns: Cirencester, Cheltenham, Gloucester.

Access: From Cirencester, I prefer the A429 (which includes a left turn half a mile out of Cirencester) to where it meets the A40(T) just north of Northleach at map ref: 114156. Turn left at this roundabout and then left along the A436. About a mile further along, on your left, a road leads directly to Withington. There are shorter routes along minor roads, but they can be very narrow and mucky in places.

Parking: Entering Withington, take care at the sharp left bend around the Mill Inn, then first left into the Inn's car park. An accommodating landlord had no objections to my parking there.

Public Transport: None that I could see, but ring Gloucester County Council on 0452 425543.

Refreshments: The Mill Inn. If the landlord is good enough to offer the use his car park, one is almost duty bound, I think.

The Walk

Leave the car park [see *Parking*] and turn left at the road. Watch for traffic: there are 'double yellows' on either side, but it is only a short step to where you bear right, as indicated by the green sign: 'Jubilee Village Hall'. Continue down to the hall and then left – direction south – keeping the hall to your right – over a stile, along a dismantled railway; and left, again, at the wire fence, to the road.

Right, here, passing (and hearing) the boarding kennels, beyond which, it is a matter of about twenty yards to where you turn left, by the sign 'Woodbridge'. Go under the railway bridge, footsteps echoing, following the lane around to the right. Further on, take the signposted footpath left, over a stile, along a field, direction north-east. If you have brought fido along, several notices tell you to keep him on a lead. This is grassy walking, over a succession of stiles. There are masses of catkins in the winter months and a patch of hawthorn; on your right you can see the River Coln meandering below. Bear slightly right, walking east as far as a fading yellow arrow-head which directs right, through an open gate, down a field, in a south-east direction. Another stile and then over the river, negotiating a tree trunk of a bridge, with wire netting underfoot and a wooden rail to hand.

On the far side, do not follow the river bank – the path curves left, briefly, and then right, up the field, direction east, veering south. You will see a pink paper disc (unless 'seen off' by the elements) and several arrow-heads on trees. A stile brings you to the road.

Turn left, down to a crossroad, where you bear right, enticingly signposted 'Roman Villa and Yanworth'. Incidentally, one may avoid the crossroad by cutting across open land, saving a few yards. This is a long stretch of road; the River Coln is to your left, still meandering. Finally, bear right at the junction, walking up to Chedworth Roman Villa.

To see or not to see: that is the question ... time and inclination, really; but a couple of hours well spent in my humble opinion. You may decide to drive and visit separately. One cautionary note: parking is limited. A mass of literature is available that describes the place much better than yours truly. However, as an appetiser and in summary: Chedworth Villa

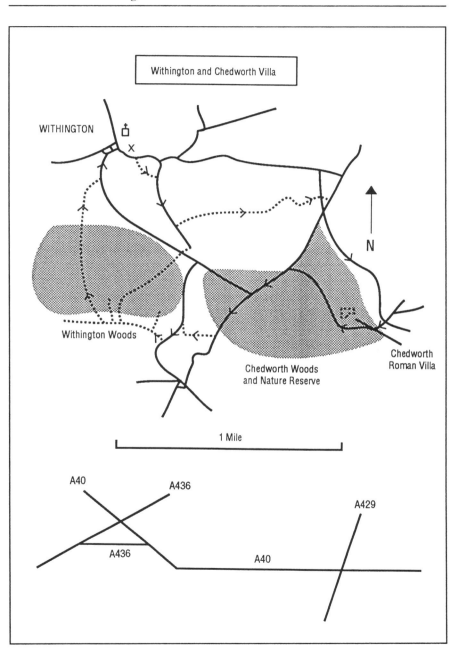

Withington and Chedworth Villa

WITHINGTON

X

N

Withington Woods

Chedworth Woods
and Nature Reserve

Chedworth
Roman Villa

1 Mile

A40
A436

A436

A40

A429

was built around 120 AD; rebuilt, added to and occupied until about 400 AD. It lies at the head of a valley surrounded by trees. The site was well chosen, for although facing the east and therefore exposed to cold winter winds, it is sheltered from the wet and windy west, has ample supplies of water and access to stone suitable for building. 'Roman' about the country was made easy, as can be seen from the map – the Fosse Way (now the A429) is only a mile or two away. There is a museum and a video programme. Run by the National Trust, the villa is open March to October, Tuesdays to Sundays and Bank Holiday Mondays. To visit at other times of the year, it is best to ring 0242 890256. Not altogether cheap: currently £2.50 per adult, £1.25 per child.

Assuming you have seen the villa, go immediately right, west, up a stony path. A few yards before the bridge, climb steps to your left (awkward spacing) that lead to the trackbed of that old railway, again. You are now in Chedworth Nature Reserve. Go right along here – not a place to walk barefoot. There are several requests to budding geologists: 'Do not hammer on this face. Samples may be taken from scree elsewhere'. Eventually, you approach a bridge – a dead end – take the path that leads left to the road; and again, left, direction south-west.

A long, but not 'too' steep ascent follows. The road levels and a footpath sign stands to your right. Up and over. Fortunately, the top two strands of barbed wire are sheathed in rubber (damage limitation). Proceed across the field – north-west – passing to the right of a Nissen hut – another stile – another field – to a gate in the corner. Go right, along a strip of tarmac to the road.

Turn left along the road – the grass verge on either side is adequate – a couple of minutes to where you bear right, opposite a letter-box, by two signs, 'Worksavers Chedworth'. Walk along the lane, past the radio mast and through a white gate. God bless America. See the US mail letter-box (approved by the Postmaster General), as you enter Withington Woods?

Continue past a house on your left, which has February's snowdrops in its back garden. Ignore the arrow-head on the tree, opposite. Walking west, there is a maze of paths to follow: this one narrows with plenty of mud to look forward to. Ignore the first track leading sharply to your right and, just beyond, keep to the right-hand path at the fork. Further on, ignore the second track to your right, but take the third, ten yards further, in a northerly direction. Proceed to a junction and keep straight on. Approaching a second junction, an arrow-head on a tree points left; ignore this, bearing right, as indicated by an arrow-head on a post on your right, not seen until actually at the junction. The track descends to a gate. Leaving the wood, go immediately left, on through a gap in the hedge. In the distance, you can see the tower of Withington's church. Follow the path down the field, under pylons, over two stiles to the road. Turn left at the road, walking around to the Church of St Michael.

Church of St Michael

St Michael's is Norman in origin and was restored in the nineteenth century. Enter through the thirteenth century south porch whose doorway is richly decorated with three chevron arches. Inside, on your left, guides, leaflets and postcards are available. In the south-west corner, high in the wall, sit the seventeenth century marble effigies of the Howes of Cassey Compton: Sir John and his wife, and their eight children, below. Walking east along the nave, you will see a fourteenth century tomb topped with pinnacles – part of the south wall. The south transept is now a Lady Chapel; its east window is by Sir Ninian Comper. On the floor of the south side of the chancel, looking positively prehistoric, but actually dating from the fourteenth century, lies the stone effigy of a priest.

Leaving the church, bear left along the road, again keeping a wary eye open for traffic, down to the Mill Inn, where a sharp left brings you back to the car park and the start of the walk.

24. Hampnett, Stowell and Yanworth

Healthy exercise in glorious Gloucestershire, cunningly disguised as an appreciation of ecclesiastic art. A walk of about five miles and a look at three churches along the way, each with wall paintings, from old to relatively new, to admire. Having parked in front of the Church of St George, Hampnett [see Parking], a browse around church number one seems a good idea.

Route: Hampnett – Yanworth – Stowell – Hampnett

Distance: About 5 miles

Map: O.S. Landranger 163

Start: See *Parking*

Terrain: Generally, quite good. Some mud, of course, and one ascent approaching Stowell.

Nearest Towns: Cirencester, Cheltenham, Gloucester

Access: From Cirencester, take the A429 towards Stow-on-the-Wold (not forgetting the left turn half a mile out of Cirencester) to where it ascends out of Northleach. Half way up the hill, take the minor road left. Hampnett is a mile or so further on.

Parking: There is a handy area of grass in front of the church in Hampnett.

Public Transport: None that I could see, but ring Gloucester County Council on 0452 425543.

Refreshments: Take a flask!

Norman in origin with fifteenth century additions, St George's in Hampnett was restored in 1868. Go through the south porch and you will see a painting of the Last Supper hanging on the north wall, opposite; but it is the feast of wall paintings that arrest rather than catch the eye. They surround the windows along the nave and cover the chancel. 'Executed' by the Reverend W. Wiggin and dating from around 1871 – the chancel, in particular, looks unusual, to say the least.

The Chancel, Church of St George, Hampnett

The Walk

So much for art; for now, anyway. Back across the grass to the road, where you go left a few yards and then take the lane opposite, direction south, a signposted public path. On your left, you can see the tower of the Church of St Peter and St Paul at Northleach; not included in this walk, however. Continue down the wide, unsurfaced lane, ignoring the crossing footpath. Pass a farm building (plenty of mud, here) and the lane veers west and eventually opens onto a field. Make for the telegraph pole in the centre, then bear left – west – those with twenty-twenty vision should be able to make out a stile in the hedge. Head up to the stile and cross it, keeping the hedge to your right. Proceed along the field to a gate, which must be climbed, and the road.

Cross with care, taking the road opposite, signposted: 'Fossebridge and Coln St Dennis', walking south for about twenty yards to where you turn sharp right along another unsurfaced lane. Further on, you may

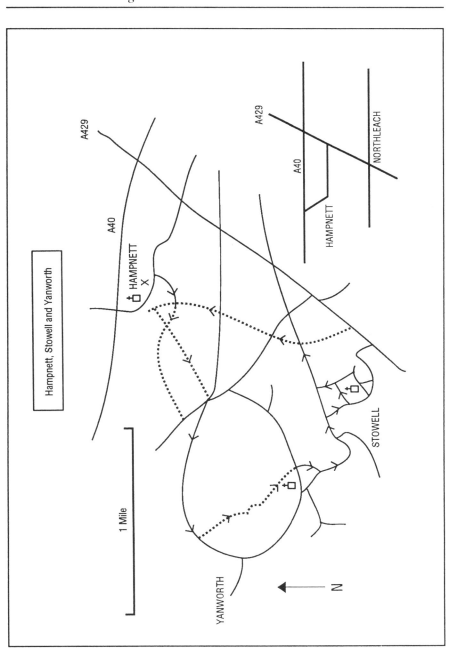

discover muddy mud edging stealthily up the sides of your boots. This is a long stretch along high ground – the lane is joined by another, curves left and descends to crossing pylons.

Here, bear left, direction south-east, passing under the pylons. The surface gives way to grass, winds to right and left, and eventually rises to the far side of the valley. There are fine views all around. Finally, you reach a barn, part of Church Farm, where you turn right, past the farm office, on to Yanworth's Church of St Michael.

The squat, battlemented tower is topped by a wafer-thin rooster that blows to and fro in the wind. St Michael's dates from the twelfth century. Inside, on your left, at the west end – more wall paintings, interesting although somewhat faded. The one on the north side of the west wall depicts a skeletal Father Time. Walking down the nave and into the transept, you may care to squint along the squint to the altar. Ever had the feeling that you are being watched? Well, look up and you will see many stone faces gazing down. A word, also, in praise of the kneelers: bright, attractive colours and patterns; a pleasure to kneel on.

Leaving the church, bear left a few yards and then take the road south-east, past stables to a junction. Right, here, and then left at the next junction. The narrow road curves left sharply and ascends – some real exercise at last. Nearing the top of the hill, take the road right, signed: 'STRICTLY PRIVATE – NO THROUGH ROAD'. Daunting block capitals; but as a pedestrian, you can at least make a short detour to look at the church. Continue south-east to another sign: 'SLOW – HORSES, CHILDREN, DOGS'. What about walkers? Follow the road around and up the steps to the Church of St Leonard, Stowell.

With origins back in Norman times, St Leonard's underwent restoration in 1898. Through the twelfth century doorway and you will see a wall painting on the north wall. Not a 'happy' theme, it represents doom – catastrophe, the Last Judgement – and dates from the twelfth century. Walking east along the nave, you can see scraps of more paintings on the south wall of the south transept and a piscina in its south-east corner. Also, there is a thirteenth century piscina in the south-east corner of the chancel.

Returning to the road, you may care to note, in passing, the imposing Stowell Park Mansion. It was built at the beginning of the sixteenth century for Sir Robert Atkins. Battlements on one side; terraced lawns on the other; an old red phone box, too.

Do not continue left on leaving the church, for you will be trespassing (as I was politely advised), but retrace your steps to the 'SLOW ...' sign. Here, proceed north-east, through a gate, along a strip of grass to another gate. Through (obviously), then left at the road to the 'main' road, where you go right, resuming your original route. Further on – a bridleway – saddle the horse and ride left, direction north. Approaching the road, you go literally under a pylon (look up and feel dizzy). Cross and continue, passing to the left of Stowell Reservoirs. More fields to a more substantial road. Again, cross, through a gate, down what is now officially a public path. See the tower of Hampnett's church on the horizon? One last gate (a patchy zebra 'colour' – lift the loop of wire) and down to where you join the first lane. Bear right, back up to the church and the start of the walk.

25. Coates and Rodmarton

A busy walking itinerary, with much to see: starting in the car park beside the Tunnel House (an inn), visiting the tunnel entrance (a canal), passing through the villages of Coates, Rodmarton and Tarlton, looking at two churches and observing the wildlife in Hailey Wood.

Route: Coates – Hailey Wood – Rodmarton – Tarlton – Coates

Distance: About 7 miles

Map: O.S. Landranger 163

Start: See Parking

Terrain: Not at all bad, and not as muddy as I had expected, especially through Hailey Wood. Famous last words? Wear your boots. The weather was dry and unusually warm for March.

Nearest Towns: Cirencester, Stroud, Tetbury.

Access: Along the A433 Tetbury to Cirencester road, take the signposted road to Tarlton at map ref: 979985. In Tarlton, take the first right – signposted: 'Coates and Cirencester', and then go left at the Tunnel House sign. Drive slowly – the lane has a rough surface, stony with potholes.

Parking: Further along this lane, you come to the Tunnel House. The grassy car park is on your left.

Public Transport: Ring Gloucester County Council on 0452 425543. I saw a bus stop sign in Coates and another in Rodmarton. It should, therefore, be possible to 'bus it', joining the walk in either village.

Refreshments: The Tunnel House. They have guest beers from time to time, so you may strike it lucky and see your favourite tipple. But only a pint if you are driving. They also serve Theakston's – their 'Old Peculier' is a powerful brew. Half a pint, I think.

The Walk

Leaving the car park, take the steps down to the entrance of Sapperton Tunnel. The stone face of the tunnel arch has certainly seen better days. Forming part of the Thames and Severn canal, the tunnel was completed in 1789 and used from that date until 1911. An Inland Waterways map gives the length as 3808 yards. Ever tried walking along a canal, upside down? There was no room to take a horse through the tunnel, and the bargees used to lie on their backs and propel their boats by 'walking' their legs along the tunnel walls. It is possible to take a boat trip inside, but unfortunately, at the time of writing, anyway, such trips have been suspended due to low water levels. All one can do is shout and listen to the echo. For the latest information ring 0666 502797.

The entrance to Sapperton Tunnel, near Coates

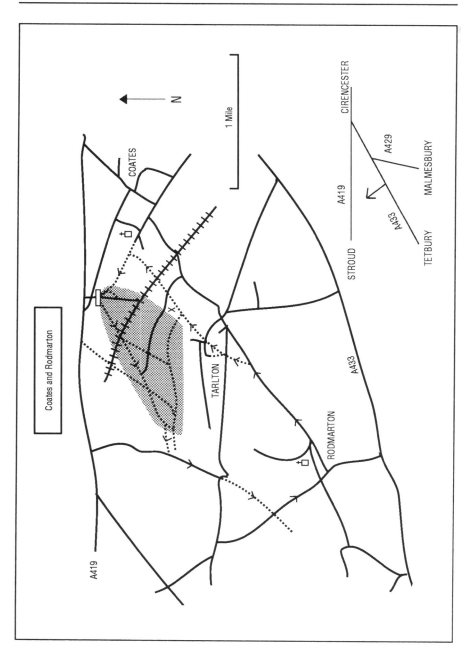

Back up the steps and turn right, to where the lane curves right, taking the signposted footpath over a stile and across the railway line. Please note the 'BEWARE OF TRAINS' warning – this is a busy main line. Proceed along the grass strip across a field – a church tower lies dead ahead. On through a gap in the hedge and across another field, past Church Farm and then bear right, through the churchyard, to the Church of St Matthew, Coates.

Walk around to your left, noting the pinnacled and battlemented four-teenth century tower, and enter via the south porch. The arch above the doorway is Norman; in fact, St Matthew's dates from Norman times and was restored in 1861. Inside, to your left, on the west wall, are several seventeenth and eighteenth century brasses of various shapes and sizes. Near the south-east corner of the south wall is a thirteenth century piscina. There is also a beautiful stained glass window in the east wall behind the altar which dates from 1876. Leave the church, but go right, this time – the 'browse' is not over yet. Stand back and look at the west wall of the tower. Focus on a point several feet above the door and window, towards the right-hand corner. Yes ... cannibalism ... an anthropophagus, holding its victim by the legs, in the process of swallowing him whole. An impressive upper row of stone teeth.

Return to Church Farm and take the right-hand path, direction north-west. A 'Landowners Welcome Caring Walkers' arrow-head shows the way. Further on, you should see another arrow-head on a telegraph pole as you walk along the edge of a field towards Hailey Wood. At the entrance to the wood there is a disc but no arrow-head. Go through, and then almost immediately right, along a track, direction north. Bear left between workshops – a sawmill, smell the wood – and just beyond a shed with the sign: 'NO UNAUTHORISED PERSONS', left, again, taking the track direction south, veering south-west, deep into the heart of Hailey Wood. This is pleasant walking, despite the ominous scattering of feathers on the ground. Shades of Berkeley – I saw a pale yellow butterfly on a warm March day. Keep to the main track, over the railway bridge, bearing right, and arriving at a clearing – seven choices of route – as ever, straight on, south-west. Finally, the track descends to the left. Here, go straight on to a padlocked gate and walk around the fence (a yard or two to your right), leaving the wood, following the path between two fields to a lane. Left, here; further along, a muddy patch can be easily avoided by making a short detour.

At the road, go straight on, and where the road curves left, again, straight on, along the footpath, south-west. A narrow, twisting path – watch for brambles. It continues beyond the next road, but here, go left, a 'short haul' to Rodmarton, passing a Neighbourhood Watch sign, to a crossroad. Take the road signposted: 'Rodmarton and Tarlton', walking east, as far as the Church of St Peter, Rodmarton.

What variety – the church path is lined with Thuja Rheingold (I think), variegated yews and a variegated holly. On the wall beyond the south porch, two gargoyles stare down below battlements. Above, stands a fourteenth century tower and spire topped by an 'off-green' rooster. St Peter's was restored twice in the latter half of the nineteenth century. Inside, you will see a large notice giving a brief history of the church; an old milk churn, too, with a slot in the top, inviting donations. 'Milking' the visitors? Never. A look around the church is worth a contribution ... fifty pence? A pound? Walking along the nave, the wood of the pulpit is sixteenth century. On the south wall of the chancel there is a fine brass to John Edward (1461). According to the leaflet, his daughter married the great nephew of Dick Whittington. History is everywhere, as is more beautiful stained glass, particularly in the east window.

Leaving the church, go down to the road and turn left, past the letter-box and bus shelter, Rodmarton School and a house with two 'bird topiaries' in its garden. A long stretch to Tarlton and a signposted footpath – left, direction north, just before the houses. The gate does not open easily and is best climbed. At the road, you are presented with a choice of two paths – take the right-hand one – through the gate, walking across a field, making for a point a few yards to the left of a telegraph pole in the opposite hedge. Two stiles – the first is a 'high-stepper' – to a field, and on to where you climb some wood strung between two posts. Surprisingly, you are now in someone's back garden. Go around the shed to the wall and follow it to the front gate.

Bear left at the road and along for twenty yards or so; then right, through a gate. A signposted footpath – north-east – across two fields to an old stone stile. The railing is easily pulled back and replaced. This stops the inquisitive horse that followed me from getting out. Continue north-east; from this higher position, the remainder of the walk to the Tunnel House is visible.

Church of St Peter, Rodmarton

Keep just to the right of a line of telegraph poles, down to the corner of the field, ignoring the entrance to Hailey Wood (a bridleway on the map) and seeking the stone stile set in the hedge. There is no sign, and it can be missed. Over, and up a strip of grass along a last field, still north-east, back to the start of the walk.

Background Readings on Rural Gloucestershire

Robert Dover

Robert Dover was born at Great Ellingham, Norfolk, in 1582. He entered Queens' College, Cambridge, at the tender age of 13, but did not take a degree. Eventually, Dover became a law student at Gray's Inn, London, and went on from there to practise law. He married Sibella Sanford, a widow, who bore him four children: two girls – Abigail and Sibella, and two boys – John and Robert. Unfortunately, Robert, born in 1616, died later that same year.

And what, you may wonder, does such a man – a Norfolk man at that – have to do with Gloucestershire? Well, walk the Cotswold Way between Chipping Campden and Broadway and there is your answer; for you will cross Dover's Hill, the site of the Cotswold 'Olympick' Games.

In 1612, give or take a year, soon after his move to Saintbury, Robert Dover began to take an interest in the Cotswold Games. They had been held since Saxon times, on the Thursday and Friday after Whitsun. Dover took them over when they were still rather crude, both in organisation and content. He improved the games beyond measure, ultimately, to the point where they attracted the nobility and gentry of the Cotswolds – not only to take part in the many 'sports' on offer, but also to attend as an important social event.

Hence, the upper layers of society, people of gentle birth and good breeding, suitably attired in all their finery, could 'see and be seen' – indulging, perhaps, in a spot of hunting, while in between, catching up on the latest gossip, eating, drinking and generally making merry.

Dover's games also enjoyed the patronage of James I. The King gave Dover a 'royal suit', complete with hat and feather. A showman, really; he must have been an impressive sight, presiding over his beloved games, resplendent, astride a white horse. To further enliven the proceedings, Dover had erected a castle in miniature, built of wood, from which guns were fired at intervals.

The games themselves were diverse, yet hardly the Olympic Games of today. The participants could wrestle, dance, throw the hammer, leapfrog, hunt, course and race horses. To add a modicum of culture, tents were erected in which cards and chess were played.

Some of the more physical activities were not for the faint-hearted. Singlestick fighting, for example, where men squared up to one another – stick in one hand – the other thrust into their belts. They then belayed each other about the head. Cotswold men, naturally enough, were famous for their prowess. In those days, being called a 'Cotswold man' was praise indeed.

Robert Dover was a popular man of his day; and what better proof of this than the publication in 1636 of the Annalia Dubrensia? Essentially, a small book of poems praising Dover and his games. Many well known poets contributed, including Ben Jonson, the English dramatist and critic.

The games prospered under Dover's management, but all good things must come to an end. Charles I raised his standard at Nottingham on 22nd August, 1642; and so began the Civil War between Cavaliers and Roundheads.

Dover's twilight years were spent at Barton-on-the-Heath, Warwickshire, where he died in 1652, at the ripe old age of seventy. Dover's Hill was left to the sheep, and the Puritans held sway over the land.

The games were revived after the Restoration, when the monarchy in the person of Charles II was re-established. They deteriorated somewhat in the succeeding years and ended in 1853. Dover's Hill is now the property of the National Trust, yet his name, surely, will live on forever.

Domesday Book

In 1085, William the Conqueror sent commissioners to each shire in the land. Their brief was to take evidence on oath 'from the Sheriff (the Crown's chief executive officer in a county); from all the barons and their Frenchmen; and from the whole Hundred, the priests, the reeves (chief magistrates) and six villagers from each village'. William also sent a second set of commissioners 'to check shires they did not know, where they were themselves unknown, to check their predecessors' survey, and report culprits to the King.'

Thoroughness went hand in hand with promptness; in less than one year, Domesday Book, a record of the survey of England was completed. Its purpose was to assess land tax and other dues, determine the value of crown lands, and enable the king to estimate the power of his vassal barons.

Lands in dispute were also listed. Domesday Book was more than a tax assessment – it was also the final authoritative register of rightful possession, so that every 'man should know his right and not usurp another's'.

The entries usually answered the commissioners' questions, arranged in five main groups:

1. The place and its holder, its *hides* (a land unit reckoned as 120 acres), ploughs and lordship.

2. People.

3. Resources.

4. Value.

5. Additional notes.

Villages were grouped into administrative districts called Hundreds, which formed regions within Shires, or Counties, many of which survive today.

Essentially a stocktaking, concise and to the point, Domesday Book uniquely describes eleventh century England under William's rule. Consider, for example, the village of Brimpsfield in the hundred of Rapsgate in Gloucestershire. A sample entry for Brimpsfield reads as follows:

'Land of Osbern Giffard in Rapsgate Hundred Osbern also holds Brimpsfield. 9 hides which pay tax. Dunn held it from Earl Harold. In lordship 3 ploughs; 16 villagers, 6 smallholders and a priest with 12 ploughs. 8 male and 4 female slaves; 2 mills at 64d.

In Gloucester 5 burgesses at 2s. The value is and was £12.'

The translation into English from eleventh century Latin was a task confined to specialists. Impossible to be exact – some words are obsolete, others have changed their meaning.

Feudal England – a hierarchy of power and obligation, from the monarch downwards. How times have changed: the old shillings and pence are with us no longer; and what about the entry '8 male and 4 female slaves'? A hard life, for some.

Wales has its Commotes, England, its Hundreds. Since then, of course, new Counties have sprung into existence – one such being Avon, which swallowed chunks of the old Gloucestershire. But don't despair, at the time of writing it is rumoured that still more boundary changes are possible; Avon, in particular, may disappear.

In a lighter vein, why not add your Hundred to your address, and totally confuse (or delight) the postman?

Reproduced by kind permission from the Phillimore edition of *Domesday Book* (General Editor John Morris), volume 15 Gloucestershire (County Editor John S. Moore), published in 1982 by Phillimore & Co. Ltd., Shopwyke Hall, Chichester, West Sussex.

Rural Gloucestershire

These are extracts from William Marshall's *Rural Gloucestershire of the Eighteenth Century* ... of Cider, Victualling the Harvest Men, and the Dairy.

Cider: Today, the price of a pint of cider is of arm and leg proportions; and although a barrel of scrumpy may be obtained quite cheaply from farms, that, too, will change if the EEC has its way. Consider Gloucestershire, two hundred years ago – a different world.

Marshall had few kind words for the labourers. He allowed that: 'Their wages are very low, in money, being only 1s. a day.' But then went on: '... in drink, shamefully exhorbitant.' This depends on one's point of view, I suppose. Marshall quoted a daily allowance of six quarts (twelve pints); but this was a minimum, to wet one's whistle: '... frequently two gallons; sometimes nine or ten quarts; or an unlimited quantity.'

In a 'fruit year', with cider cheap and plentiful: 'It is no uncommon circumstance to send out a general invitation, into the highways and hedges; in order to empty the casks which were filled, last year, that they may be refilled this.' Heady stuff, in more ways than one. Marshall continued: 'A habit of drinking is not easily corrected. Nor is an art learnt in youth readily forgotten.' He related several stories – drinking exploits, which he considered incredible. 'Drinking a gallon-bottle-full, at a draught, is said to be no uncommon feat: a mere boyish trick. Another man of the vale undertook, for a trifling wager, to drink twenty pints. He 'got down' nineteen (as the story is gravely told) but these filling the cask to the bung, the twentieth could not of course get admittance.'

Mind-boggling? Maybe; but a bagatelle compared to the masters. 'Four well-seasoned yeomen, having raised their courage with the juice of the apple, resolved to have a fresh hogshead tapped; and, setting foot to foot, emptied it at one sitting.'

Victualling the Harvest Men: Wages at that time were 'thirty shillings for the harvest; or a shilling a day with full board.' It was 'the method of victualling' that Marshall found 'singularly judicious'. 'They have no regular dinner. Their breakfast is cold meat. Their refreshment, in the field, bread and cheese, with six or eight quarts of beverage. At night, when they return home, a hot supper; and, after it, each man a quart of strong liquor; in order to alleviate the fatigues of the day which is past; and, by sending him to bed in spirits and good humour, to prepare him for the morrow's toil.'

One assumes that no pun was intended with the words 'in spirits'. Fatigued they certainly were, for the morrow's toil was toil, indeed; and they worked very long hours, 'from dawn to dusk'.

Talking to 'an active good husbandman', Marshall quoted the man as saying: 'Lord, Sir, what should we do now, (about noon), if we were to give our men a regular dinner! They must either go home to it; or we must bring it to them here, in the field; and while they were eating, and playing under the hedge, we should lose the hauling of two or three load of beans.'

The Dairy: Marshall described 'this arduous department' as being under the control of the 'Mistress of the Dairy', though sometimes an 'experienced Dairy Maid' was the manager. He had nothing but praise: 'With respect to cleanliness, the Gloucestershire dairywomen stand unimpeachable. Judging from the dairies I have seen, they are much above par. A cheese dairy is a manufactury – a workshop – and is, in truth, a place of hard work. That studied outward neatness which is to be seen in the show dairies of different districts may be in character where butter is the only object. But it would be superfluous in a cheese dairy. The scalding brush, only, can give the requisite sweetness: and I have seen it no where more diligently used, than in Gloucestershire. Cleanliness implies industry. A Gloucestershire dairywoman is hard at work, from four o'clock in the morning until bed time.'

Imagine, travelling back in time and having to choose – labourer or harvest man, probably. A dairy maid? Well, the change of sex would be somewhat traumatic, I think; but far worse – having to get up at four in the morning – impossible. I would be poor, but the 'juice of the apple' would be freely available by way of consolation. Then, again, a 'well seasoned yeoman', slightly higher up the social scale, would be better still; though emptying a hogshead in the company of three friends might prove difficult.

Reproduced by kind permission from *The Rural Economy of Gloucestershire* by William Marshall, published by Alan Sutton Publishing Ltd., Phoenix Mill, Far Thrupp, Stroud, Gloucestershire.